AIR FRYER TOASTER OVEN COMBO COOKBOOK FOR BEGINNERS

1000-DAYS CRISPY AND JUICY AFFORDABLE RECIPES FOR STAY ON A BUDGET

LYNN GROSS

Copyright © 2021 by Lynn Gross- All rights reserved.

The content contained within this book may not be reproduced, duplicated, or transmitted without direct written permission from the author or the publisher. Under no circumstances will any blame or legal responsibility be held against the publisher, or author, for any damages, reparation, or monetary loss due to the information contained within this book, either directly or indirectly.

Legal Notice: This book is copyright protected. It is only for personal use. You cannot amend, distribute, sell, use, quote or paraphrase any part, or the content within this book, without the consent of the author or publisher.

Disclaimer Notice: Please note the information contained within this document is for educational and entertainment purposes only. All effort has been executed to present accurate, up to date, reliable, complete information. No warranties of any kind are declared or implied. Readers acknowledge that the author is not engaged in the rendering of legal, financial, medical, or professional advice. The content within this book has been derived from various sources. Please consult a licensed professional before attempting any techniques outlined in this book. By reading this document, the reader agrees that under no circumstances is the author responsible for any losses, direct or indirect, that are incurred as a result of the use of the information contained within this document, including, but not limited to, errors, omissions, or inaccuracies.

CONTENTS

INTRODUCTION 7
- How the Air Fryer Oven Works 7
- The Benefits of the Air Fryer Oven 7
- The Preparations for the Air Fryer Oven 7
- How to Clean Your Air Fryer Oven 8

BREAKFAST 10
- Apple Incredibles 10
- Mushroom-spinach Frittata With Feta 11
- Lemon Blueberry Scones 12
- Turkey And Tuna Melt 13
- Flaky Granola 14
- Walnut Pancake 15
- Garlic Parmesan Bread Ring 16
- New York–style Crumb Cake 17
- Spinach, Tomato & Feta Quiche 18
- Baked Curried Fruit 19
- Chocolate Chip Banana Muffins 20
- Strawberry Pie Glaze 21
- Brown Sugar Grapefruit 22

VEGETABLES AND VEGETARIAN 23
- Brussels Sprouts 23
- Roasted Veggie Kebabs 24
- Oregano Zucchini 25
- Chilaquiles 26
- Roasted Herbed Shiitake Mushrooms 27
- Lemon-glazed Baby Carrots 28
- Pecan Parmesan Cauliflower 29
- Roasted Brussels Sprouts With Bacon 30
- Buttery Rolls 31
- Zucchini Boats With Ham And Cheese 32

- Roasted Ratatouille Vegetables 33
- Air-fried Potato Salad 34
- Stuffed Onions 35

LUNCH AND DINNER 36
- Oven-baked Barley 36
- Kashaburgers 37
- Parmesan Artichoke Pizza 38
- Easy Oven Lasagne 39
- French Bread Pizza 40
- Italian Stuffed Zucchini Boats 41
- Crab Chowder 42
- Harvest Chicken And Rice Casserole 43
- Oven-baked Couscous 44
- Parmesan Crusted Tilapia 45
- Yeast Dough For Two Pizzas 46
- Sheet Pan Beef Fajitas 47
- Chicken Gumbo 48

FISH AND SEAFOOD 49
- Cajun Flounder Fillets 49
- Maple Balsamic Glazed Salmon 50
- Spicy Fish Street Tacos With Sriracha Slaw 51
- Tortilla-crusted Tilapia 52
- Beer-breaded Halibut Fish Tacos 53
- Horseradish Crusted Salmon 54
- Shrimp Patties 55
- Quick Shrimp Scampi 56
- Stuffed Baked Red Snapper 57
- Shrimp Po'boy With Remoulade Sauce 58
- Popcorn Crawfish 59
- Tasty Fillets With Poblano Sauce 60
- Shrimp, Chorizo And Fingerling Potatoes 61

SNACKS APPETIZERS AND SIDES 62

Ham And Cheese Palmiers 62
Panko-breaded Onion Rings 63
Cauliflower-crust Pizza 64
Shrimp Pirogues 65
Crispy Tofu Bites 66
Middle Eastern Phyllo Rolls 67
Baked Spinach + Artichoke Dip 68
Wonton Cups 69
Crab Rangoon 70
Harissa Roasted Carrots 71
Caramelized Onion Dip 72
Corn Dog Muffins 73
Bacon Bites 74

POULTRY 75

Tasty Meat Loaf 75
Fiesta Chicken Plate 76
Tender Chicken Meatballs 77
Guiltless Bacon 78
Fried Chicken 79
Crispy Fried Onion Chicken Breasts 80
Chicken Schnitzel Dogs 81
Pecan Turkey Cutlets 82
Chicken Potpie 83
Italian Baked Chicken 84
Tandoori Chicken Legs 85
Chicken Adobo 86
Sesame Chicken Breasts 87

DESSERTS 88

Blueberry Cookies 88
Giant Buttery Oatmeal Cookie 89
Pineapple Tartlets 90
Baked Apple 91
Strawberry Blueberry Cobbler 92

Maple-glazed Pumpkin Pie 93
Coconut Rice Pudding 94
Orange-glazed Brownies 95
Giant Oatmeal–peanut Butter Cookie 96
Freezer-to-oven Chocolate Chip Cookies 97
Campfire Banana Boats 98
Pear And Almond Biscotti Crumble 99
Cinnamon Sugar Rolls 100

BEEF PORK AND LAMB 101
Italian Sausage & Peppers 101
Lamb Koftas Meatballs 102
Cilantro-crusted Flank Steak 103
Crunchy Fried Pork Loin Chops 104
Kielbasa Chunks With Pineapple & Peppers 105
Indian Fry Bread Tacos 106
Kielbasa Sausage With Pierogies And Caramelized Onions 107
Perfect Strip Steaks 108
Barbecue-style London Broil 109

INTRODUCTION

How the Air Fryer Oven Works

An air fryer works by rapidly circulating hot air and a small amount of oil to fry foods. The oil and air work in tandem, transferring heat both via conduction (the direct contact of the hot oil) and convection (the heavy rotation of hot air). In a wall oven or the oven of a range with convection, the air fry function works the same way.

The Benefits of the Air Fryer Oven

An air frying oven uses little to no oil to create a flavorful and crunchy texture on foods and boasts all of the same benefits as a standalone air fryer - with some additional conveniences.

The air fry feature is integrated right into your oven, eliminating the need to store an extra appliance or take up valuable counter space.

An air frying oven has more capacity, saving you time and allowing you to cook more food at once so that there's always enough for the whole family.

An air fry oven does more than just air fry, so one appliance works harder for you. Enjoy other features such as Even Baking with True Convection, Fast Steam Cleaning, and Smudge-Proof Stainless Steel.

The Preparations for the Air Fryer Oven

1. Find the right place for your air fryer oven in your kitchen. Make sure you have some clearance around the oven so that the hot air can escape from the vent at the back.
2. Preheat your air fryer before adding your food. Because an air fryer heats up so quickly, it isn't critical to wait for the oven to preheat before putting food inside, but it's a good habit to get into. Sometimes a recipe requires a hot start and putting food into a less than hot oven will give you less than perfect results. For instance, pastry bakes better if cold pastry is placed into a hot oven. Pizza dough works better with a burst of heat at the beginning of baking. It only takes a few minutes to preheat the oven, so unless you're in a real rush, just wait to put your food inside.
3. Invest in a kitchen spray bottle. Spraying oil on the food is easier than drizzling or brushing, and allows you to use less oil overall. It will be worth it!
4. Think about lining your drip tray with aluminum foil for easy clean up.

How to Clean Your Air Fryer Oven

After we have all the basic knowledge about the air fryer toaster ovens, let's discuss the very common question; how to clean a Cuisinart convection toaster oven, or how to clean a convection toaster oven? Following is a list of ways to clean it:

Clean it with homemade dish soap cleaner

For the best and safe cleaning, it is necessary to unplug your toaster oven and disconnect the apparatus from the force source before you start cleaning.

Also, obviously, never inundate it in water. After that, put the toaster oven on a bit of paper to get the pieces, then take out the metal plate, rack, and lower scrap plate and spot them in the sink. Then, use dish soap and water to wash these parts.

To battle any difficult stains on these removable pieces, and let them dry totally while you clean the remainder of the machine.

The next step is to make your own cleaning answer for the inside of the toaster oven by consolidating vinegar, warm water, and a little dish soap. Apply that to the inside with a clammy wipe.

However, do whatever it takes not to get any of the fluid on the warming components. Some toaster ovens have a porcelain polish or a nonstick inside that makes them marginally simpler to clean.

In any case, it very well may be harmed by metal scouring cushions and rough cleaners. You can utilize a wipe, material, or old cloth when cleaning down your toaster oven.

Clean it with baking soda

You might get surprised to know that how to clean a toaster oven with baking soda. Let us tell you the process in detail:

Baking Soda is incredible for cleaning since its normally antacid nature artificially responds to water and vinegar, which makes dirt and oil break down rapidly and without any problem.

Baking soda is an all-common substance present in every living thing. While the vast majority know it for baking, it's properties are extraordinary for a wide assortment of things.

It likewise has an incredible rough quality if not weakened excessively, so it's an extraordinary option in contrast to other markets since baking soda is an incredibly protected and powerful cleaning item.

Also, baking soda is totally non-poisonous and protected to use around food, children, and pets. You can also clean the heating component in your toaster oven by utilizing a gentle soap and a clean, buildup free cloth on a cool, unplugged toaster oven.

Tenderly wipe the loops guaranteeing no buildup from the cleaning cloth remains. Also, it is normal to have water and soap on the cloth; however, try not to get the radiator component significantly wet.

However, if we don't clear every ounce of buildup off, you'll get that delightful toasted baking soda smell whenever you use it. For another, we would prefer not to chance to harm the component, driving you to purchase another one.

Therefore, keep in mind that we have to unplug the toaster oven and do nothing until it's totally cool. Then, take a wipe or material in some warm water. Then start delicately cleaning the length of the warming component to and fro.

If you're following our entire how to clean a toaster oven with baking soda steps, this should be the first thing you do. As we said toward the beginning, try not to utilize soap or different cleaners on the warming components as they could harm it.

Try to let everything dry first prior to stopping the toaster oven back in or utilizing it. To clean a toaster oven with baking soda, make a glue with baking soda and water. In a cool, unplugged toaster oven, spread the glue within the oven, dodging the warming components.

Let it sit for 12 hours or more. For minor cleaning, 1 hour should do the trick, and then wipe clean with a soggy fabric and warm water. After that, we are well aware of the cleaning methods; let us understand the best way to turn off the digital air fryer.

BREAKFAST

Apple Incredibles

Servings: 6

Cooking Time: 25 Minutes

Ingredients:
- Muffin mixture:
- 2 cups unbleached flour
- 1 teaspoon baking powder
- ¼ cup brown sugar
- ½ teaspoon salt
- ¼ cup margarine, at room temperature
- ½ cup skim milk
- 1 egg, beaten
- 2 tablespoons finely chopped raisins
- 2 tablespoons finely chopped pecans
- 1 apple, peeled, cored, and thinly sliced

Directions:
1. Preheat the toaster oven to 400° F.
2. Combine the muffin mixture ingredients in a large bowl, stirring just to blend. Fill the pans of an oiled or nonstick 6-muffin tin with the batter. Insert the apple slices vertically into the batter, standing and pushing them all the way down to the bottom of the pan.
3. BAKE for 25 minutes, or until the apples are tender and the muffins are lightly browned.

Mushroom-spinach Frittata With Feta

Servings: 4

Cooking Time: 35 Minutes

Ingredients:

- 1 tablespoon olive oil
- 1 cup white mushrooms, chopped
- 1 shallot, finely chopped
- 1 teaspoon minced garlic
- 4 large eggs
- ½ cup milk
- ½ cup fresh baby spinach, shredded
- 1 tablespoon fresh basil, chopped
- ⅛ teaspoon sea salt
- ⅛ teaspoon freshly ground black pepper
- ¾ cup feta cheese, crumbled

Directions:

1. Place the baking tray on position 1 and preheat the toaster oven on BAKE to 350°F for 5 minutes.
2. Add the oil to an 8-inch-square baking dish, tilting the dish to coat the bottom.
3. Combine the mushrooms, shallot, and garlic in the baking dish. Bake the vegetables for 5 minutes or until softened, stirring halfway through.
4. While the vegetables are cooking, in a large bowl, whisk the eggs, milk, spinach, basil, salt, and pepper.
5. Take the baking dish out of the oven and pour in the egg mixture, stirring slightly to evenly disperse the vegetables.
6. Top the frittata with the feta cheese and bake for 30 minutes. The frittata should be puffy and golden, and a knife inserted in the center should come out clean.
7. Cool for 5 minutes and serve.

Lemon Blueberry Scones

Servings: 6

Cooking Time: 25 Minutes

Ingredients:
- 1 ½ cups all-purpose flour
- 2 tablespoons granulated sugar
- 2 ¼ teaspoons baking powder
- 1 teaspoon grated lemon zest
- ¼ teaspoon table salt
- ¼ cup unsalted butter, cut into 1-tablespoon pieces
- ¾ cup fresh or frozen blueberries
- ¾ cup plus 1 tablespoon heavy cream, plus more for brushing
- Coarse white sugar
- LEMON GLAZE
- 1 cup confectioners' sugar
- 2 to 3 tablespoons fresh lemon juice

Directions:
1. Line a 12 x 12-inch baking pan with parchment paper.
2. Whisk the flour, granulated sugar, baking powder, lemon zest, and salt in a large bowl. Cut in the butter using a pastry cutter or two knives until the mixture is crumbly throughout. Gently stir in the blueberries, taking care not to mash them. Add ¾ cup cream and gently stir until a soft dough forms. If needed, stir in an additional tablespoon of cream so all of the flour is moistened.
3. Turn the dough onto a lightly floured board. Pat the dough into a circle about ¾ inch thick and 6 inches in diameter. Cut into 6 triangles. Arrange the triangles on the prepared pan. Freeze for 15 minutes.
4. Preheat the toaster oven to 400°F. Brush the scones lightly with cream and sprinkle with coarse sugar. Bake for 20 to 25 minutes or until golden brown. Let cool for 5 minutes.
5. Meanwhile, make the glaze: Stir the confectioners' sugar and lemon juice in a small bowl, blending until smooth. Drizzle the glaze over the scones. Let stand for about 5 minutes. These taste best served freshly made and slightly warm.

Turkey And Tuna Melt

Servings: 2

Cooking Time: 4 Minutes

Ingredients:

- 4 slices multigrain bread Spicy brown mustard
- 1 6-ounce can tuna in water, drained well and crumbled
- ¼ pound thinly sliced turkey breast
- 4 slices low-fat Monterey Jack cheese
- 2 tablespoons finely chopped scallions
- Salt and freshly ground black pepper

Directions:

1. Spread one side of each bread slice with mustard and place on an oiled or nonstick
2. 6½ × 10-inch baking sheet.
3. Layer 2 slices with equal portions of tuna, turkey, cheese, and scallion. Season to taste with salt and pepper.
4. TOAST twice, or until the cheese is melted.

Flaky Granola

Servings: 3
Cooking Time: 20 Minutes

Ingredients:
- ¼ cup rolled oats
- ½ cup wheat flakes
- ½ cup bran flakes
- ¼ cup wheat germ
- 3 tablespoons sesame seeds
- 4 ¼ cup unsweetened shredded coconut
- ½ cup chopped almonds, walnuts, or pecans
- 2 tablespoons chopped pumpkin seeds
- ½ cup honey or molasses
- 2 tablespoons vegetable oil
- Salt to taste

Directions:
1. Preheat the toaster oven to 375° F.
2. Combine all the ingredients in a medium bowl, stirring to mix well.
3. Spread the mixture in an oiled or nonstick 6½ × 6½ × 2-inch square (cake) pan.
4. BAKE for 20 minutes, turning with tongs every 5 minutes to toast evenly. Cool and store in an airtight container in the refrigerator.

Walnut Pancake

Servings: 4

Cooking Time: 20 Minutes

Ingredients:
- 3 tablespoons butter, divided into thirds
- 1 cup flour
- 1½ teaspoons baking powder
- ¼ teaspoon salt
- 2 tablespoons sugar
- ¾ cup milk
- 1 egg, beaten
- 1 teaspoon pure vanilla extract
- ½ cup walnuts, roughly chopped
- maple syrup or fresh sliced fruit, for serving

Directions:
1. Place 1 tablespoon of the butter in air fryer oven baking pan. Air-fry at 330°F for 3 minutes to melt.
2. In a small dish or pan, melt the remaining 2 tablespoons of butter either in the microwave or on the stove.
3. In a medium bowl, stir together the flour, baking powder, salt, and sugar. Add milk, beaten egg, the 2 tablespoons of melted butter, and vanilla. Stir until combined but do not beat. Batter may be slightly lumpy.
4. Pour batter over the melted butter in air fryer oven baking pan. Sprinkle nuts evenly over top.
5. Air-fry for 20 minutes or until toothpick inserted in center comes out clean. Turn air fryer oven off, close the machine, and let pancake rest for 2 minutes.
6. Remove pancake from pan, slice, and serve with syrup or fresh fruit.

Garlic Parmesan Bread Ring

Servings: 6   Cooking Time: 30 Minutes

Ingredients:

- ½ cup unsalted butter, melted
- ¼ teaspoon salt (omit if using salted butter)
- ¾ cup grated Parmesan cheese
- 3 to 4 cloves garlic, minced
- 1 tablespoon chopped fresh parsley
- 1 pound frozen bread dough, defrosted
- olive oil
- 1 egg, beaten

Directions:

1. Combine the melted butter, salt, Parmesan cheese, garlic and chopped parsley in a small bowl.
2. Roll the dough out into a rectangle that measures 8 inches by 17 inches. Spread the butter mixture over the dough, leaving a half-inch border un-buttered along one of the long edges. Roll the dough from one long edge to the other, ending with the un-buttered border. Pinch the seam shut tightly. Shape the log into a circle sealing the ends together by pushing one end into the other and stretching the dough around it.
3. Cut out a circle of aluminum foil that is the same size as the air fryer oven. Brush the foil circle with oil and place an oven safe ramekin or glass in the center. Transfer the dough ring to the aluminum foil circle, around the ramekin. This will help you make sure the dough will fit in the baking pan and maintain its ring shape. Use kitchen shears to cut 8 slits around the outer edge of the dough ring halfway to the center. Brush the dough ring with egg wash.
4. Preheat the toaster oven to 400°F for 4 minutes. When it has preheated, brush the baking pan with oil and transfer the dough ring, foil circle and ramekin into the baking pan. Slide the drawer back into the air fryer oven, but do not turn the air fryer oven on. Let the dough rise inside the warm air fryer oven for 30 minutes.
5. After the bread has proofed in the air fryer oven for 30 minutes, set the temperature to 340°F and air-fry the bread ring for 15 minutes. Flip the bread over by inverting it onto a plate or cutting board and sliding it back into the air fryer oven. Air-fry for another 15 minutes. Let the bread cool for a few minutes before slicing the bread ring in between the slits and serving warm.

New York–style Crumb Cake

Servings: 8 Cooking Time: 90 Minutes

Ingredients:
- CRUMB TOPPING
- 8 tablespoons unsalted butter, melted
- ⅓ cup (2⅓ ounces) granulated sugar
- ⅓ cup packed (2⅓ ounces) dark brown sugar
- ¾ teaspoon ground cinnamon
- ⅛ teaspoon table salt
- 1¾ cups (7 ounces) cake flour
- CAKE
- 1¼ cups (5 ounces) cake flour
- ½ cup (3½ ounces) granulated sugar
- ¼ teaspoon baking soda
- ¼ teaspoon table salt
- 6 tablespoons unsalted butter, cut into 6 pieces and softened
- ⅓ cup buttermilk
- 1 large egg plus 1 large yolk
- 1 teaspoon vanilla extract
- Confectioners' sugar

Directions:

1. Adjust toaster oven rack to middle position and preheat the toaster oven to 325 degrees. Make foil sling for 8-inch square baking pan by folding 2 long sheets of aluminum foil so each is 8 inches wide. Lay sheets of foil in pan perpen-dicular to each other, with extra foil hanging over edges of pan. Push foil into corners and up sides of pan, smoothing foil flush to pan.

2. FOR THE CRUMB TOPPING: Whisk melted butter, granulated sugar, brown sugar, cinnamon, and salt in medium bowl until combined. Add flour and stir with rubber spatula or wooden spoon until mixture resembles thick, cohesive dough; set aside to cool to room temperature, 10 to 15 minutes.

3. FOR THE CAKE: Using stand mixer fitted with paddle, mix flour, sugar, baking soda, and salt on low speed to combine. With mixer running, add softened butter 1 piece at a time. Continue beating until mixture resembles moist crumbs with no visible butter pieces remaining, 1 to 2 minutes. Add buttermilk, egg and yolk, and vanilla and beat on medium-high speed until light and fluffy, about 1 minute, scraping down bowl as needed.

4. Transfer batter to prepared pan. Using rubber spatula, spread batter into even layer. Break apart crumb topping into large pea-size pieces and sprinkle in even layer over batter, beginning with edges and then working toward center. (Assembled cake can be wrapped tightly with plastic wrap and refrigerated for up to 24 hours; increase baking time to 40 to 45 minutes.)

5. Bake until crumbs are golden and toothpick inserted in center of cake comes out clean, 35 to 40 minutes, rotating pan halfway through baking. Let cool on wire rack for at least 30 minutes. Using foil overhang, lift cake out of pan. Dust with confectioners' sugar before serving.

Spinach, Tomato & Feta Quiche

Servings: 8   Cooking Time: 60 Minutes

Ingredients:

- Pie Crust Ingredients
- 1½ cups all-purpose flour, plus more for dusting
- ½ teaspoon kosher salt
- 3 tablespoons unsalted butter, chilled and cubed
- 6 tablespoons vegetable shortening, chilled
- 3 tablespoons ice water
- Dry beans or uncooked rice, for filling

- Filling Ingredients
- 1½ ounces frozen spinach, thawed and squeezed dry
- 9 cherry tomatoes, halved
- 1½ ounces crumbled feta cheese 4 large eggs
- ½ cup heavy cream
- ½ teaspoon kosher salt
- ¼ teaspoon freshly ground black pepper
- Extra virgin olive oil, for drizzling

Directions:

1. Combine the flour and salt in a food processor and pulse once to combine.
2. Add the butter and shortening, then pulse until the mixture creates fine crumbs.
3. Pour the water in slowly and pulse until it forms a dough.
4. Form the dough into a square, wrap with plastic wrap, and place in the fridge for 6 hours or overnight.
5. Remove the dough from the fridge, unwrap it, and place onto a lightly floured work surface.
6. Roll out the dough into a 10-inch diameter circle. You may need to use additional flour to keep the dough from sticking to the rolling pin.
7. Place the dough into the tart pan and use your fingers to form the dough to fit the pan.
8. Trim the edges and prick the bottom of the tart shell all over.
9. Cover with plastic wrap and place in the freezer for 30 minutes.
10. Remove from the freezer, unwrap, and top with parchment paper that covers all the edges.
11. Fill the tart shell with dry beans or uncooked rice until the dough is fully covered. Set aside.
12. Preheat the toaster Oven to 350°F.
13. Place the tart shell on the wire rack, then insert the rack at low position in the preheated oven.
14. Select the Bake function, press the Fan/Light button to start the fan, then press Start/Pause.
15. Remove the tart shell from the oven and let it cool for 1 hour.
16. Arrange the spinach, tomatoes, and feta cheese evenly inside the empty tart shell.
17. Whisk together the eggs, heavy cream, salt, and pepper until well combined.

18. Pour the egg mixture into the filled tart shell and lightly drizzle with extra-virgin olive oil. You may have some extra filling left over.
19. Preheat the toaster Oven to 350°F.
20. Place the quiche on the wire rack, then insert the rack at low position in the preheated oven.
21. Select the Bake function, then press Start/Pause.
22. Remove the quiche from the oven and let it cool for 5 minutes.
23. Cut into slices and serve.

Baked Curried Fruit

Servings: 4　　　　　　　　　　　　　　　　Cooking Time: 25 Minutes

Ingredients:
- Curry mixture:
- 2 tablespoons dry white wine
- 1 teaspoon lemon juice
- ¼ teaspoon ground allspice
- ¼ teaspoon ground ginger
- ¼ teaspoon ground cardamom
- ¼ teaspoon turmeric
- ¼ teaspoon ground cumin
- ¼ teaspoon ground coriander
- Pinch of grated nutmeg
- Pinch of cayenne
- 2 tablespoons honey
- 1 teaspoon soy sauce
- 1 16-ounce can pear halves, drained
- 1 8-ounce can pineapple chunks, drained
- 1 16-ounce can peach halves

Directions:
1. Preheat the toaster oven to 350° F.
2. Combine the curry mixture ingredients in a 1-quart 8½ × 8½ × 4-inch ovenproof baking dish and add the fruit, mixing well.
3. BAKE, uncovered, for 25 minutes, or until bubbling and the sauce is thickened. Cool and serve on a sesame wafer with Creamy Yogurt Sauce.

Chocolate Chip Banana Muffins

Servings: 12

Cooking Time: 14 Minutes

Ingredients:
- 2 medium bananas, mashed
- ¼ cup brown sugar
- 1½ teaspoons vanilla extract
- ⅔ cup milk
- 2 tablespoons butter
- 1 large egg
- 1 cup white whole-wheat flour
- ½ cup old-fashioned oats
- 1 teaspoon baking soda
- ½ teaspoon baking powder
- ⅛ teaspoon sea salt
- ¼ cup mini chocolate chips

Directions:
1. Preheat the toaster oven to 330°F.
2. In a large bowl, combine the bananas, brown sugar, vanilla extract, milk, butter, and egg; set aside.
3. In a separate bowl, combine the flour, oats, baking soda, baking powder, and salt.
4. Slowly add the dry ingredients into the wet ingredients, folding in the flour mixture ⅓ cup at a time.
5. Mix in the chocolate chips and set aside.
6. Using silicone muffin liners, fill 6 muffin liners two-thirds full. Carefully place the muffin liners in the air fryer oven and bake for 20 minutes (or until the tops are browned and a toothpick inserted in the center comes out clean). Carefully remove the muffins from the air fryer oven and repeat with the remaining batter.
7. Serve warm.

Strawberry Pie Glaze

Servings: 2

Cooking Time: 15 Minutes

Ingredients:

- ½ cup apple juice
- 2 tablespoons sugar
- 1 teaspoon lemon or lime juice

Directions:

1. Combine all the ingredients in an oiled or nonstick 8½ × 8½ × 2-inch square baking (cake) pan.
2. BROIL for 6 minutes, or until the sugar is melted. Carefully remove from the oven using oven mitts, stir to blend, then broil again for 6 minutes, or until the liquid is reduced and clear. Remove from the oven and brush the strawberries immediately with the glaze. Chill before serving.

Brown Sugar Grapefruit

Servings: 2

Cooking Time: 4 Minutes

Ingredients:

- 1 grapefruit
- 2 to 4 teaspoons brown sugar

Directions:

1. Preheat the toaster oven to 400°F.
2. While the air fryer oven is Preheating, cut the grapefruit in half horizontally (in other words not through the stem or blossom end of the grapefruit). Slice the bottom of the grapefruit to help it sit flat on the counter if necessary. Using a sharp paring knife (serrated is great), cut around the grapefruit between the flesh of the fruit and the peel. Then, cut each segment away from the membrane so that it is sitting freely in the fruit.
3. Sprinkle 1 to 2 teaspoons of brown sugar on each half of the prepared grapefruit. Set up a rack in the air fryer oven (use an air fryer oven rack or make your own rack with some crumpled up aluminum foil). You don't have to use a rack, but doing so will get the grapefruit closer to the element so that the brown sugar can caramelize a little better. Transfer the grapefruit half to the rack in the air fryer oven. Depending on how big your grapefruit are and what size air fryer oven you have, you may need to do each half separately to make sure they sit flat.
4. Air-fry at 400°F for 4 minutes.
5. Remove and let it cool for just a minute before enjoying.

VEGETABLES AND VEGETARIAN

Brussels Sprouts

Servings: 3

Cooking Time: 5 Minutes

Ingredients:
- 1 10-ounce package frozen brussels sprouts, thawed and halved
- 2 teaspoons olive oil
- salt and pepper

Directions:
1. Toss the brussels sprouts and olive oil together.
2. Place them in the air fryer oven and season to taste with salt and pepper.
3. Air-fry at 360°F for approximately 5 minutes, until the edges begin to brown.

Roasted Veggie Kebabs

Servings: 4

Cooking Time: 45 Minutes

Ingredients:
- Brushing mixture:
- 3 tablespoons olive oil
- 1 tablespoon soy sauce
- 1 teaspoon garlic powder
- 1 teaspoon ground cumin
- 2 tablespoons balsamic vinegar
- Salt and freshly ground black pepper to taste
- Cauliflower, zucchini, onion, broccoli, bell pepper, mushrooms, celery, cabbage, beets, and the like, cut into approximately 2 × 2-inch pieces

Directions:
1. Preheat the toaster oven to 400° F.
2. Combine the brushing mixture ingredients in a small bowl, mixing well. Set aside.
3. Skewer the vegetable pieces on 4 9-inch metal skewers and place the skewers lengthwise on a broiling rack with a pan underneath.
4. BAKE for 40 minutes, or until the vegetables are tender, brushing with the mixture every 10 minutes.
5. BROIL for 5 minutes, or until lightly browned.

Oregano Zucchini

Servings: 4

Cooking Time: 30 Minutes

Ingredients:

- Mixture:
- 3 tablespoons olive oil
- 1 tablespoon Roasted Garlic
- 2 tablespoons tomato paste
- 2 tablespoons dry white wine
- 1 tablespoon chopped fresh oregano
- Salt and freshly ground pepper to taste
- 4 small zucchini squash, rinsed well, halved, then quartered
- 3 tablespoons grated Parmesan cheese

Directions:

1. Whisk together the mixture ingredients in a small bowl, adjusting the seasonings to taste. Add the zucchini and toss gently to coat well. Transfer to an oiled or nonstick 8½ × 8½ × 2-inch square baking (cake) pan.

2. Broil, uncovered, for 20 minutes. Remove the pan from the oven, turn the pieces with tongs, and spoon the sauce over the zucchini. Broil again for 10 minutes, or until tender. Before serving, sprinkle with the grated Parmesan cheese.

Chilaquiles

Servings: 4

Cooking Time: 25 Minutes

Ingredients:
- Oil spray (hand-pumped)
- 1¼ cups store-bought salsa
- 1 (15-ounce) can low-sodium navy or black beans, drained and rinsed
- ½ cup corn kernels
- ¼ cup chicken broth
- ¼ sweet onion, chopped
- ½ teaspoon minced garlic
- 25 tortilla chips, broken up into 2-inch pieces
- 1½ cups queso fresco cheese, crumbled
- 1 avocado, chopped
- 1 scallion, white and green parts, chopped

Directions:
1. Place the rack in position 1 and preheat the toaster oven to 400°F on BAKE for 5 minutes.
2. Lightly coat an 8-inch-square baking dish with oil spray and set aside.
3. In a large bowl, stir the salsa, beans, corn, chicken broth, onion, and garlic until well mixed.
4. Add the tortilla chips and stir to combine. It is okay if the tortilla chips break up a little.
5. Transfer the mixture to the baking dish, top with the cheese, and cover tightly with foil.
6. Bake for 20 minutes until the chips are soft, the mixture is bubbly, and then uncover and bake until the cheese is golden and melted, about 5 minutes.
7. Serve topped with the avocado and scallion.

Roasted Herbed Shiitake Mushrooms

Servings: 5

Cooking Time: 4 Minutes

Ingredients:

- 8 ounces shiitake mushrooms, stems removed and caps roughly chopped
- 1 tablespoon olive oil
- ½ teaspoon salt
- freshly ground black pepper
- 1 teaspoon chopped fresh thyme leaves
- 1 teaspoon chopped fresh oregano
- 1 tablespoon chopped fresh parsley

Directions:

1. Preheat the toaster oven to 400°F.
2. Toss the mushrooms with the olive oil, salt, pepper, thyme and oregano. Air-fry for 5 minutes. The mushrooms will still be somewhat chewy with a meaty texture. If you'd like them a little more tender, add a couple of minutes to this cooking time.
3. Once cooked, add the parsley to the mushrooms and toss. Season again to taste and serve.

Lemon-glazed Baby Carrots

Servings: 4

Cooking Time: 33 Minutes

Ingredients:
- Glaze:
- 1 tablespoon margarine
- 2 tablespoons lemon juice
- 1 tablespoon honey
- 1 teaspoon garlic powder
- Salt and freshly ground black pepper to taste
- 2 cups peeled baby carrots (approximately 1 pound)
- 1 tablespoon chopped fresh parsley or cilantro

Directions:

1. Place the glaze ingredients in a 1-quart 8½ × 8½ × 4-inch ovenproof baking dish and broil for 4 minutes, or until the margarine is melted. Remove from the oven and mix well. Add the carrots and toss to coat. Cover the dish with aluminum foil.

2. BAKE, covered, at 350° F. for 30 minutes, or until the carrots are tender. Garnish with chopped parsley or cilantro and serve immediately.

Pecan Parmesan Cauliflower

Servings: 4

Cooking Time: 35 Minutes

Ingredients:

- 2½ cups (frozen thawed or fresh) thinly sliced cauliflower florets
- Salt and freshly ground black pepper
- 3 tablespoons freshly grated Parmesan cheese
- ½ cup ground pecans

Directions:

1. Preheat the toaster oven to 400° F.
2. Combine the florets and oil in a 1-quart 8½ × 8½ × 4-inch ovenproof baking dish, tossing to coat well. Season to taste with salt and pepper. Cover the dish with aluminum foil.
3. BAKE for 25 minutes, or until tender. Uncover and sprinkle with the cheese and pecans.
4. BROIL for 10 minutes, or until lightly browned.

Roasted Brussels Sprouts With Bacon

Servings: 20

Cooking Time: 4 Minutes

Ingredients:

- 4 slices thick-cut bacon, chopped (about ¼ pound)
- 1 pound Brussels sprouts, halved (or quartered if large)
- freshly ground black pepper

Directions:

1. Preheat the toaster oven to 380°F.
2. Air-fry the bacon for 5 minutes.
3. Add the Brussels sprouts to the air fryer oven and drizzle a little bacon fat from the pan into the air fryer oven. Toss the sprouts to coat with the bacon fat. Air-fry for an additional 15 minutes, or until the Brussels sprouts are tender to a knifepoint.
4. Season with freshly ground black pepper.

Buttery Rolls

Servings: 6   Cooking Time: 14 Minutes

Ingredients:

- 6½ tablespoons Room-temperature whole or low-fat milk
- 3 tablespoons plus 1 teaspoon Butter, melted and cooled
- 3 tablespoons plus 1 teaspoon (or 1 medium egg, well beaten) Pasteurized egg substitute, such as Egg Beaters
- 1½ tablespoons Granulated white sugar
- 1¼ teaspoons Instant yeast
- ¼ teaspoon Table salt
- 2 cups, plus more for dusting All-purpose flour
- Vegetable oil
- Additional melted butter, for brushing

Directions:

1. Stir the milk, melted butter, pasteurized egg substitute (or whole egg), sugar, yeast, and salt in a medium bowl to combine. Stir in the flour just until the mixture makes a soft dough.
2. Lightly flour a clean, dry work surface. Turn the dough out onto the work surface. Knead the dough for 5 minutes to develop the gluten.
3. Lightly oil the inside of a clean medium bowl. Gather the dough into a compact ball and set it in the bowl. Turn the dough over so that its surface has oil on it all over. Cover the bowl tightly with plastic wrap and set aside in a warm, draft-free place until the dough has doubled in bulk, about 1½ hours.
4. Punch down the dough, then turn it out onto a clean, dry work surface. Divide it into 5 even balls for a small batch, 6 balls for a medium batch, or 8 balls for a large one.
5. For a small batch, lightly oil the inside of a 6-inch round cake pan and set the balls around its perimeter, separating them as much as possible.
6. For a medium batch, lightly oil the inside of a 7-inch round cake pan and set the balls in it with one ball at its center, separating them as much as possible.
7. For a large batch, lightly oil the inside of an 8-inch round cake pan and set the balls in it with one at the center, separating them as much as possible.
8. Cover with plastic wrap and set aside to rise for 30 minutes.
9. Preheat the toaster oven to 350°F.
10. Uncover the pan and brush the rolls with a little melted butter, perhaps ½ teaspoon per roll. When the machine is at temperature, set the cake pan in the air fryer oven. Air-fry undisturbed for 14 minutes, or until the rolls have risen and browned.
11. Using kitchen tongs and a nonstick-safe spatula, two hot pads, or silicone baking mitts, transfer the cake pan from the air fryer oven to a wire rack. Cool the rolls in the pan for a minute or two. Turn the rolls out onto a wire rack, set them top side up again, and cool for at least another couple of minutes before serving warm.

Zucchini Boats With Ham And Cheese

Servings: 4

Cooking Time: 12 Minutes

Ingredients:

- 2 6-inch-long zucchini
- 2 ounces Thinly sliced deli ham, any rind removed, meat roughly chopped
- 4 Dry-packed sun-dried tomatoes, chopped
- ⅓ cup Purchased pesto
- ¼ cup Packaged mini croutons
- ¼ cup (about 1 ounce) Shredded semi-firm mozzarella cheese

Directions:

1. Preheat the toaster oven to 375°F.
2. Split the zucchini in half lengthwise and use a flatware spoon or a serrated grapefruit spoon to scoop out the insides of the halves, leaving at least a ¼-inch border all around the zucchini half. (You can save the scooped out insides to add to soups and stews—or even freeze it for a much later use.)
3. Mix the ham, sun-dried tomatoes, pesto, croutons, and half the cheese in a bowl until well combined. Pack this mixture into the zucchini "shells." Top them with the remaining cheese.
4. Set them stuffing side up in the air fryer oven without touching (even a fraction of an inch between them is enough room). Air-fry undisturbed for 12 minutes, or until softened and browned, with the cheese melted on top.
5. Use a nonstick-safe spatula to transfer the zucchini boats stuffing side up on a wire rack. Cool for 5 or 10 minutes before serving.

Roasted Ratatouille Vegetables

Servings: 15

Cooking Time: 2 Minutes

Ingredients:

- 1 baby or Japanese eggplant, cut into 1½-inch cubes
- 1 red pepper, cut into 1-inch chunks
- 1 yellow pepper, cut into 1-inch chunks
- 1 zucchini, cut into 1-inch chunks
- 1 clove garlic, minced
- ½ teaspoon dried basil
- 1 tablespoon olive oil
- salt and freshly ground black pepper
- ¼ cup sliced sun-dried tomatoes in oil
- 2 tablespoons chopped fresh basil

Directions:

1. Preheat the toaster oven to 400°F.
2. Toss the eggplant, peppers and zucchini with the garlic, dried basil, olive oil, salt and freshly ground black pepper.
3. Air-fry the vegetables at 400°F for 15 minutes.
4. As soon as the vegetables are tender, toss them with the sliced sun-dried tomatoes and fresh basil and serve.

Air-fried Potato Salad

Servings: 4

Cooking Time: 15 Minutes

Ingredients:

- 1⅓ pounds Yellow potatoes, such as Yukon Golds, cut into ½-inch chunks
- 1 large Sweet white onion(s), such as Vidalia, chopped into ½-inch pieces
- 1 tablespoon plus 2 teaspoons Olive oil
- ¾ cup Thinly sliced celery
- 6 tablespoons Regular or low-fat mayonnaise (gluten-free, if a concern)
- 2½ tablespoons Apple cider vinegar
- 1½ teaspoons Dijon mustard (gluten-free, if a concern)
- ¾ teaspoon Table salt
- ¼ teaspoon Ground black pepper

Directions:

1. Preheat the toaster oven to 400°F.
2. Toss the potatoes, onion(s), and oil in a large bowl until the vegetables are glistening with oil.
3. When the machine is at temperature, transfer the vegetables to the air fryer oven, spreading them out into as even a layer as you can. Air-fry for 15 minutes, tossing and rearranging the vegetables every 3 minutes so that all surfaces get exposed to the air currents, until the vegetables are tender and even browned at the edges.
4. Pour the contents of the air fryer oven into a serving bowl. Cool for at least 5 minutes or up to 30 minutes. Add the celery, mayonnaise, vinegar, mustard, salt, and pepper. Stir well to coat. The potato salad can be made in advance; cover and refrigerate for up to 4 days.

Stuffed Onions

Servings: 6 Cooking Time: 27 Minutes

Ingredients:

- 6 Small 3½- to 4-ounce yellow or white onions
- Olive oil spray
- 6 ounces Bulk sweet Italian sausage meat (gluten-free, if a concern)
- 9 Cherry tomatoes, chopped
- 3 tablespoons Seasoned Italian-style dried bread crumbs (gluten-free, if a concern)
- 3 tablespoons (about ½ ounce) Finely grated Parmesan cheese

Directions:

1. Preheat the toaster oven to 325°F (or 330°F, if that's the closest setting).
2. Cut just enough off the root ends of the onions so they will stand up on a cutting board when this end is turned down. Carefully peel off just the brown, papery skin. Now cut the top quarter off each and place the onion back on the cutting board with this end facing up. Use a flatware spoon (preferably a serrated grapefruit spoon) or a melon baller to scoop out the "insides" (interior layers) of the onion, leaving enough of the bottom and side walls so that the onion does not collapse. Depending on the thickness of the layers in the onion, this may be one or two of those layers—or even three, if they're very thin.
3. Coat the insides and outsides of the onions with olive oil spray. Set the onion "shells" in the air fryer oven and air-fry for 15 minutes.
4. Meanwhile, make the filling. Set a medium skillet over medium heat for a couple of minutes, then crumble in the sausage meat. Cook, stirring often, until browned, about 4 minutes. Transfer the contents of the skillet to a medium bowl (leave the fat behind in the skillet or add it to the bowl, depending on your cross-trainer regimen). Stir in the tomatoes, bread crumbs, and cheese until well combined.
5. When the onions are ready, use a nonstick-safe spatula to gently transfer them to a cutting board. Increase the air fryer oven's temperature to 350°F.
6. Pack the sausage mixture into the onion shells, gently compacting the filling and mounding it up at the top.
7. When the machine is at temperature, set the onions stuffing side up in the air fryer oven with at least ¼ inch between them. Air-fry for 12 minutes, or until lightly browned and sizzling hot.
8. Use a nonstick-safe spatula, and perhaps a flatware fork for balance, to transfer the onions to a cutting board or serving platter. Cool for 5 minutes before serving.

LUNCH AND DINNER

Oven-baked Barley

Servings: 2

Cooking Time: 60 Minutes

Ingredients:
- ⅓ cup barley, toasted
- Seasonings:
- 1 tablespoon sesame oil
- 1 tablespoon sesame seeds
- ¼ teaspoon ground cumin
- ¼ teaspoon turmeric
- ½ teaspoon garlic powder
- Salt and freshly ground black pepper to taste

Directions:

1. Combine the barley and 1½ cups water in a 1-quart 8½ × 8½ × 4-inch ovenproof baking dish. Cover with aluminum foil.
2. BAKE, covered, for 50 minutes, or until almost cooked, testing the grains after 30 minutes for softness.
3. Add the oil and seasonings and fluff with a fork to combine. Cover and let the barley sit for 10 minutes to finish cooking and absorb the flavors of the seasonings. Fluff once more before serving.

Kashaburgers

Servings: 4

Cooking Time: 50 Minutes

Ingredients:

- 1 cup kasha
- 2 tablespoons minced onion or scallions
- 1 tablespoon minced garlic
- ½ cup multigrain bread crumbs
- 1 egg
- ¼ teaspoon paprika
- ½ teaspoon chili powder
- ¼ teaspoon sesame oil
- 1 tablespoon vegetable oil
- Salt and freshly ground black pepper to taste

Directions:

1. Preheat the toaster oven to 400° F.
2. Combine 2 cups water and the kasha in a 1-quart 8½ × 8½ × 4-inch ovenproof baking dish.
3. BAKE, uncovered, for 30 minutes, or until the grains are cooked. Remove from the oven and add all the other ingredients, stirring to mix well. When the mixture is cooled, shape into 4 to 6 patties and place on a rack with a broiling pan underneath.
4. BROIL for 20 minutes, turn with a spatula, then broil for another 10 minutes, or until browned.

Parmesan Artichoke Pizza

Servings: 6   Cooking Time: 15 Minutes

Ingredients:
- CRUST
- ¾ cup warm water (110°F)
- 1 ½ teaspoons active dry yeast
- ¼ teaspoon sugar
- 1 tablespoon olive oil
- 1 teaspoon table salt
- ⅓ cup whole wheat flour
- 1 ½ to 1 ⅔ cups bread flour
- TOPPINGS
- 2 tablespoons olive oil
- 1 teaspoon Italian seasoning
- 1 clove garlic, minced
- ½ cup whole milk ricotta cheese, at room temperature
- ⅔ cup drained, chopped marinated artichokes
- ¼ cup chopped red onion
- 3 tablespoons minced fresh basil
- ½ cup shredded Parmesan cheese
- ⅓ cup shredded mozzarella cheese

Directions:

1. Make the Crust: Place the warm water, yeast, and sugar in a large mixing bowl for a stand mixer. Stir, then let stand for 3 to 5 minutes or until bubbly.

2. Stir in the olive oil, salt, whole wheat flour, and 1 ½ cups bread flour. If the dough is too sticky, stir in an additional 1 to 2 tablespoons bread flour. Beat with the flat (paddle) beater at medium-speed for 5 minutes (or knead by hand for 5 to 7 minutes or until the dough is smooth and elastic). Place in a greased large bowl, turn the dough over, cover with a clean towel, and let stand for 30 to 45 minutes, or until starting to rise.

3. Stir the olive oil, Italian seasoning, and garlic in a small bowl; set aside.

4. Preheat the toaster oven to 450°F. Place a 12-inch pizza pan in the toaster oven while it is preheating.

5. Turn the dough onto a lightly floured surface and pull or roll the dough to make a 12-inch circle. Carefully transfer the crust to the hot pan.

6. Brush the olive oil mixture over the crust. Spread the ricotta evenly over the crust. Top with the artichokes, red onions, fresh basil, Parmesan, and mozzarella. Bake for 13 to 15 minutes, or until the crust is golden brown and the cheese is melted. Let stand for 5 minutes before cutting.

Easy Oven Lasagne

Servings: 4

Cooking Time: 60 Minutes

Ingredients:

- 6 uncooked lasagna noodles, broken in half
- 1 15-ounce jar marinara sauce
- ½ pound ground turkey or chicken breast
- ½ cup part-skim ricotta cheese
- ½ cup shredded part-skim mozzarella cheese
- 2 tablespoons chopped fresh oregano leaves or 1 teaspoon dried oregano
- 2 tablespoons chopped fresh basil leaves or 1 teaspoon dried basil
- 1 tablespoon garlic cloves, minced
- ¼ cup grated Parmesan cheese
- Salt and freshly ground black pepper to taste

Directions:

1. Preheat the toaster oven to 375° F.
2. Layer in a 1-quart 8½ × 8½ × 4-inch ovenproof baking dish in this order: 6 lasagna noodle halves, ½ jar of the marinara sauce, ½ cup water, half of the ground meat, half of the ricotta and mozzarella cheeses, half of the oregano and basil leaves, and half of the minced garlic. Repeat the layer, starting with the noodles. Cover the dish with aluminum foil.
3. BAKE, covered, for 50 minutes, or until the noodles are tender. Uncover, sprinkle the top with Parmesan cheese and bake for another 10 minutes, or until the liquid is reduced and the top is browned.

French Bread Pizza

Servings: 6

Cooking Time: 8 Minutes

Ingredients:
- 2 tablespoons unsalted butter, melted
- 2 cloves garlic, minced
- ½ teaspoon Italian seasoning
- 1 tablespoon olive oil
- ½ cup chopped onion
- ½ cup chopped green pepper
- 1 cup sliced button or white mushrooms
- 1 (10- to 12-ounce) loaf French or Italian bread, about 12 inches long, split in half lengthwise
- ½ cup pizza sauce
- 6 to 8 slices Canadian bacon or ¼ cup pepperoni slices
- ¼ cup sliced ripe olives, drained
- 1 cup shredded mozzarella cheese
- 3 tablespoons shredded Parmesan cheese

Directions:
1. Preheat the toaster oven to 450°F.
2. Stir the melted butter, garlic, and Italian seasoning in a small bowl; set aside.
3. Heat the oil in a small skillet over medium-high heat. Add the onion and green pepper and sauté, stirring frequently, for 3 minutes. Add the mushrooms and cook, stirring frequently, for 7 to 10 minutes or until the liquid has evaporated. Remove from the heat; set aside.
4. Gently pull a little of the soft bread out of the center of the loaf, making a well. (Take care not to tear the crust.) Brush the garlic butter over the cut sides of the bread.
5. Place both halves of the bread, side by side, cut side up, on a 12 x 12-inch baking pan. Bake for 3 minutes or until heated through. Carefully remove the bread from the oven.
6. Spoon the pizza sauce evenly over the cut sides of the bread. Top evenly with the Canadian bacon, the onion-mushroom mixture, and the olives. Top with the mozzarella and Parmesan cheeses. Return to the oven and bake for 3 to 5 minutes or until the cheese is melted.
7. Cut the French bread pizza crosswise into slices.

Italian Stuffed Zucchini Boats

Servings: 6

Cooking Time: 26 Minutes

Ingredients:

- 6 small zucchini, halved lengthwise
- 1 pound bulk hot sausage
- 1 small onion, chopped
- 2 cloves garlic, minced
- 1 small Roma tomato, seeded and chopped
- 1/4 cup Parmesan cheese
- 3 tablespoons tomato paste
- 2 teaspoons dried Italian seasoning
- 1 teaspoon salt
- 1/2 teaspoon coarse black pepper
- 1 cup shredded mozzarella cheese
- Sliced fresh basil

Directions:

1. Preheat the toaster oven to 350°F. Spray a 13x9-inch baking pan with nonstick cooking spray.
2. Scoop out center of zucchini halves. Reserve 1 1/2 cups. Place zucchini boats in baking pan.
3. In a large skillet over medium-high heat, cook sausage, stirring to crumble, about 6 minutes or until browned. Remove sausage to a medium bowl.
4. Add onion and garlic to skillet, cook until onion is translucent. Stir in reserved zucchini, sausage, tomatoes, Parmesan cheese, tomato paste, Italian seasoning, salt and black pepper.
5. Spoon mixture into the zucchini boats.
6. Bake for 20 minutes. Remove from oven and top with mozzarella cheese.
7. Bake an additional 5 to 6 minutes or until cheese is melted.
8. Sprinkle with sliced fresh basil before serving.

Crab Chowder

Servings: 4

Cooking Time: 40 Minutes

Ingredients:

- 1 6-ounce can lump crabmeat, drained and chopped, or ½ pound fresh crabmeat, cleaned and chopped
- 1 cup skim milk or low-fat soy milk
- 1 cup fat-free half-and-half
- 2 tablespoons unbleached flour
- ¼ cup chopped onion
- ½ cup peeled and diced potato
- 1 carrot, peeled and chopped
- 1 celery stalk, chopped
- 2 garlic cloves, minced
- 2 tablespoons chopped fresh parsley
- ½ teaspoon ground cumin
- 1 teaspoon paprika
- Salt and butcher's pepper to taste

Directions:

1. Preheat the toaster oven to 400° F.
2. Whisk together the milk, half-and-half, and flour in a bowl. Transfer the mixture to a 1-quart 8½ × 8½ × 4-inch ovenproof baking dish. Add all the other ingredients, mixing well. Adjust the seasonings to taste.
3. BAKE, covered, for 40 minutes, or until the vegetables are tender.

Harvest Chicken And Rice Casserole

Servings: 4

Cooking Time: 42 Minutes

Ingredients:
- 4 skinless, boneless chicken thighs, cut into 1-inch cubes
- ½ cup brown rice 4 scallions, chopped
- 1 plum tomato, chopped
- 1 cup frozen peas
- 1 cup frozen corn
- 1 cup peeled and chopped carrots
- 2 tablespoons chopped fresh parsley
- 1 teaspoon mustard seed
- 1 teaspoon dried dill weed
- ¼ teaspoon celery seed
- Salt and freshly ground black pepper to taste
- ½ cup finely chopped pecans

Directions:
1. Preheat the toaster oven to 400° F.
2. Combine all the ingredients, except the pecans, with 2½ cups water in a 1-quart 8½ × 8½ × 4-inch ovenproof baking dish. Adjust the seasonings to taste. Cover with aluminum foil.
3. BAKE, covered, for 45 minutes, or until the rice is tender, stirring after 20 minutes to distribute the liquid. When done, uncover and sprinkle the top with the pecans.
4. BROIL for 7 minutes, or until the pecans are browned.

Oven-baked Couscous

Servings: 4

Cooking Time: 10 Minutes

Ingredients:

- 1 10-ounce package couscous
- 2 tablespoons olive oil
- 2 tablespoons canned chickpeas
- 2 tablespoons canned or frozen green peas
- 1 tablespoon chopped fresh parsley
- 3 scallions, chopped
- Salt and pepper to taste

Directions:

1. Preheat the toaster oven to 400° F.
2. Mix together all the ingredients with 2 cups water in a 1-quart 8½ × 8½ × 4-inch ovenproof baking dish. Adjust the seasonings to taste. Cover with aluminum foil.
3. BAKE, covered, for 10 minutes, or until the couscous and vegetables are tender. Adjust the seasonings to taste and fluff with a fork before serving.

Parmesan Crusted Tilapia

Servings: 2

Cooking Time: 14 Minutes

Ingredients:

- 2 ounces Parmesan cheese
- 1/4 cup Italian seasoned Panko bread crumbs
- 1/2 teaspoon Italian seasoning
- 1/4 teaspoon ground black pepper
- 1 tablespoon mayonnaise
- 2 tilapia fillets or other white fish fillets (about 4 ounces each)

Directions:

1. Preheat the toaster oven to 425°F. Spray baking pan with nonstick cooking spray.
2. Using a spiralizer, grate Parmesan cheese and place in a large resealable plastic bag. Add Panko bread crumbs, Italian seasoning and black pepper. Seal and shake bag.
3. Spread mayonnaise on both sides of fish fillets. Add fish to bag and shake until coated with crumb mixture.
4. Press remaining crumbs from bag onto fish. Place on prepared baking pan.
5. Bake until fish flakes easily with a fork, 12 to 14 minutes.

Yeast Dough For Two Pizzas

Servings: 8

Cooking Time: 20 Minutes

Ingredients:

- ¼ cup tepid water
- 1 cup tepid skim milk
- ½ teaspoon sugar
- 1 1¼-ounce envelope dry yeast
- 2 cups unbleached flour
- 1 tablespoon olive oil

Directions:

1. Preheat the toaster oven to 400° F.
2. Combine the water, milk, and sugar in a bowl. Add the yeast and set aside for 3 to 5 minutes, or until the yeast is dissolved.
3. Stir in the flour gradually, adding just enough to form a ball of the dough.
4. KNEAD on a floured surface until the dough is satiny, and then put the dough in a bowl in a warm place with a damp towel over the top. In 1 hour or when the dough has doubled in bulk, punch it down and divide it in half. Flatten the dough and spread it out to the desired thickness on an oiled or nonstick 9¾-inch-diameter pie pan. Spread with Homemade Pizza Sauce (recipe follows) and add any desired toppings.
5. BAKE for 20 minutes, or until the topping ingredients are cooked and the cheese is melted.

Sheet Pan Beef Fajitas

Servings: 3

Cooking Time: 10 Minutes

Ingredients:
- Nonstick cooking spray
- 3 tablespoons olive oil
- 1 ½ teaspoons chili powder
- 2 teaspoons ground cumin
- 1 teaspoon kosher salt
- 1 onion, halved and sliced into ¼-inch strips
- 1 large red or green bell pepper, cut into thin strips
- ¾-pound flank steak, cut across the grain into thin strips
- 3 tablespoons fresh lime juice
- 3 cloves garlic, minced
- 6 flour or corn tortillas, warmed

Directions:
1. Position the rack to broil. Preheat the toaster oven on the Broil setting. Spray a 12 x 12-inch baking pan with nonstick cooking spray.
2. Combine the olive oil, chili powder, cumin, and salt in a small bowl. Add the onion and bell pepper and toss to coat them evenly with the mixture. Use a slotted spoon to remove the vegetables from the seasoned oil mixture. Reserve the seasoned oil mixture. Place the vegetables in a single layer on the prepared pan. Broil for about 5 minutes or until the vegetables are beginning to brown.
3. Meanwhile, toss the steak strips in the reserved seasoned oil mixture. Push the vegetables to one side of the pan and add the steak in a single layer on the other side of the pan. Broil for 5 minutes.
4. When the meat is done, remove the meat from the pan and toss with the lime juice and garlic. Serve the meat and vegetables in warm tortillas.

Chicken Gumbo

Servings: 4

Cooking Time: 40 Minutes

Ingredients:
- 2 skinless, boneless chicken breast halves, cut into 1-inch cubes
- ½ cup dry red wine
- 1 small onion, finely chopped
- 1 celery stalk, finely chopped
- 2 plum tomatoes, chopped
- 3 1 bell pepper, chopped
- 1 tablespoon minced fresh garlic
- 2 okra pods, stemmed, seeded, and finely chopped 1 bay leaf
- ½ teaspoon hot sauce
- ½ teaspoon dried thyme
- Salt and freshly ground black pepper to taste

Directions:
1. Preheat the toaster oven to 400° F.
2. Combine all the ingredients in a 1-quart 8½ × 8½ × 4-inch ovenproof baking dish. Adjust the seasonings to taste. Cover with aluminum foil.
3. BAKE, covered, for 40 minutes, or until the onion, pepper, and celery are tender. Discard the bay leaf before serving.

FISH AND SEAFOOD

Cajun Flounder Fillets

Servings: 2

Cooking Time: 5 Minutes

Ingredients:

- 2 4-ounce skinless flounder fillet(s)
- 2 teaspoons Peanut oil
- 1 teaspoon Purchased or homemade Cajun dried seasoning blend

Directions:

1. Preheat the toaster oven to 400°F.
2. Oil the fillet(s) by drizzling on the peanut oil, then gently rubbing in the oil with your clean, dry fingers. Sprinkle the seasoning blend evenly over both sides of the fillet(s).
3. When the machine is at temperature, set the fillet(s) in the air fryer oven. If working with more than one fillet, they should not touch, although they may be quite close together, depending on the air fryer oven's size. Air-fry undisturbed for 5 minutes, or until lightly browned and cooked through.
4. Use a nonstick-safe spatula to transfer the fillets to a serving platter or plate(s). Serve at once.

Maple Balsamic Glazed Salmon

Servings: 4

Cooking Time: 10 Minutes

Ingredients:

- 4 (6-ounce) fillets of salmon
- salt and freshly ground black pepper
- vegetable oil
- ¼ cup pure maple syrup
- 3 tablespoons balsamic vinegar
- 1 teaspoon Dijon mustard

Directions:

1. Preheat the toaster oven to 400°F.
2. Season the salmon well with salt and freshly ground black pepper. Spray or brush the bottom of the air fryer oven with vegetable oil and place the salmon fillets inside. Air-fry the salmon for 5 minutes.
3. While the salmon is air-frying, combine the maple syrup, balsamic vinegar and Dijon mustard in a small saucepan over medium heat and stir to blend well. Let the mixture simmer while the fish is cooking. It should start to thicken slightly, but keep your eye on it so it doesn't burn.
4. Brush the glaze on the salmon fillets and air-fry for an additional 5 minutes. The salmon should feel firm to the touch when finished and the glaze should be nicely browned on top. Brush a little more glaze on top before removing and serving with rice and vegetables, or a nice green salad.

Spicy Fish Street Tacos With Sriracha Slaw

Servings: 2   Cooking Time: 5 Minutes

Ingredients:
- Sriracha Slaw:
- ½ cup mayonnaise
- 2 tablespoons rice vinegar
- 1 teaspoon sugar
- 2 tablespoons sriracha chili sauce
- 5 cups shredded green cabbage
- ¼ cup shredded carrots
- 2 scallions, chopped
- salt and freshly ground black pepper
- Tacos:
- ½ cup flour
- 1 teaspoon chili powder
- ½ teaspoon ground cumin
- 1 teaspoon salt
- freshly ground black pepper
- ½ teaspoon baking powder
- 1 egg, beaten
- ¼ cup milk
- 1 cup breadcrumbs
- 1 pound mahi-mahi or snapper fillets
- 1 tablespoon canola or vegetable oil
- 6 (6-inch) flour tortillas
- 1 lime, cut into wedges

Directions:
1. Start by making the sriracha slaw. Combine the mayonnaise, rice vinegar, sugar, and sriracha sauce in a large bowl. Mix well and add the green cabbage, carrots, and scallions. Toss until all the vegetables are coated with the dressing and season with salt and pepper. Refrigerate the slaw until you are ready to serve the tacos.
2. Combine the flour, chili powder, cumin, salt, pepper and baking powder in a bowl. Add the egg and milk and mix until the batter is smooth. Place the breadcrumbs in shallow dish.
3. Cut the fish fillets into 1-inch wide sticks, approximately 4-inches long. You should have about 12 fish sticks total. Dip the fish sticks into the batter, coating all sides. Let the excess batter drip off the fish and then roll them in the breadcrumbs, patting the crumbs onto all sides of the fish sticks. Set the coated fish on a plate or baking sheet until all the fish has been coated.
4. Preheat the toaster oven to 400°F.
5. Spray the coated fish sticks with oil on all sides. Spray or brush the inside of the air fryer oven with oil and transfer the fish to the air fryer oven. Place as many sticks as you can in one layer, leaving a little room around each stick. Place any remaining sticks on top, perpendicular to the first layer.
6. Air-fry the fish for 3 minutes. Turn the fish sticks over and air-fry for an additional 2 minutes.

7. While the fish is air-frying, warm the tortilla shells either in a 350°F oven wrapped in foil or in a skillet with a little oil over medium-high heat for a couple minutes. Fold the tortillas in half and keep them warm until the remaining tortillas and fish are ready.

8. To assemble the tacos, place two pieces of the fish in each tortilla shell and top with the sriracha slaw. Squeeze the lime wedge over top and dig in.

Tortilla-crusted Tilapia

Servings: 4

Cooking Time: 12 Minutes

Ingredients:
- 4 (5-ounce) tilapia fillets
- ½ teaspoon ground cumin
- Sea salt, for seasoning
- 1 cup tortilla chips, coarsely crushed
- Oil spray (hand-pumped)
- 1 lime, cut into wedges

Directions:
1. Preheat the toaster oven to 375°F on BAKE for 5 minutes.
2. Line the baking tray with parchment paper.
3. Lightly season the fish with the cumin and salt.
4. Press the tortilla chips onto the top of the fish fillets and place them on the baking sheet.
5. Lightly spray the fish with oil.
6. In position 2, bake until golden and just cooked through, about 12 minutes in total.
7. Serve with the lime wedges.

Beer-breaded Halibut Fish Tacos

Servings: 4   Cooking Time: 10 Minutes

Ingredients:
- 1 pound halibut, cut into 1-inch strips
- 1 cup light beer
- 1 jalapeño, minced and divided
- 1 clove garlic, minced
- ¼ teaspoon ground cumin
- ½ cup cornmeal
- ¼ cup all-purpose flour
- 1¼ teaspoons sea salt, divided
- 2 cups shredded cabbage
- 1 lime, juiced and divided
- ¼ cup Greek yogurt
- ¼ cup mayonnaise
- 1 cup grape tomatoes, quartered
- ½ cup chopped cilantro
- ¼ cup chopped onion
- 1 egg, whisked
- 8 corn tortillas

Directions:
1. In a shallow baking dish, place the fish, the beer, 1 teaspoon of the minced jalapeño, the garlic, and the cumin. Cover and refrigerate for 30 minutes.
2. Meanwhile, in a medium bowl, mix together the cornmeal, flour, and ½ teaspoon of the salt.
3. In large bowl, mix together the shredded cabbage, 1 tablespoon of the lime juice, the Greek yogurt, the mayonnaise, and ½ teaspoon of the salt.
4. In a small bowl, make the pico de gallo by mixing together the tomatoes, cilantro, onion, ¼ teaspoon of the salt, the remaining jalapeño, and the remaining lime juice.
5. Remove the fish from the refrigerator and discard the marinade. Dredge the fish in the whisked egg; then dredge the fish in the cornmeal flour mixture, until all pieces of fish have been breaded.
6. Preheat the toaster oven to 350°F.
7. Place the fish in the air fryer oven and spray liberally with cooking spray. Air-fry for 6 minutes, flip the fish, and cook another 4 minutes.
8. While the fish is cooking, heat the tortillas in a heavy skillet for 1 to 2 minutes over high heat.
9. To assemble the tacos, place the battered fish on the heated tortillas, and top with slaw and pico de gallo. Serve immediately.

Horseradish Crusted Salmon

Servings: 2
Cooking Time: 14 Minutes

Ingredients:

- 2 (5-ounce) salmon fillets
- salt and freshly ground black pepper
- 2 teaspoons Dijon mustard
- ½ cup panko breadcrumbs
- 2 tablespoons prepared horseradish
- ½ teaspoon finely chopped lemon zest
- 1 tablespoon olive oil
- 1 tablespoon chopped fresh parsley

Directions:

1. Preheat the toaster oven to 360°F.
2. Season the salmon with salt and freshly ground black pepper. Then spread the Dijon mustard on the salmon, coating the entire surface.
3. Combine the breadcrumbs, horseradish, lemon zest and olive oil in a small bowl. Spread the mixture over the top of the salmon and press down lightly with your hands, adhering it to the salmon using the mustard as "glue".
4. Transfer the salmon to the air fryer oven and air-fry at 360°F for 14 minutes (depending on how thick your fillet is) or until the fish feels firm to the touch. Sprinkle with the parsley.

Shrimp Patties

Servings: 4

Cooking Time: 10 Minutes

Ingredients:
- ½ pound shelled and deveined raw shrimp
- ¼ cup chopped red bell pepper
- ¼ cup chopped green onion
- ¼ cup chopped celery
- 2 cups cooked sushi rice
- ½ teaspoon garlic powder
- ½ teaspoon Old Bay Seasoning
- ½ teaspoon salt
- 2 teaspoons Worcestershire sauce
- ½ cup plain breadcrumbs
- oil for misting or cooking spray

Directions:

1. Finely chop the shrimp. You can do this in a food processor, but it takes only a few pulses. Be careful not to overprocess into mush.
2. Place shrimp in a large bowl and add all other ingredients except the breadcrumbs and oil. Stir until well combined.
3. Preheat the toaster oven to 390°F.
4. Shape shrimp mixture into 8 patties, no more than ½-inch thick. Roll patties in breadcrumbs and mist with oil or cooking spray.
5. Place 4 shrimp patties in air fryer oven and air-fry at 390°F for 10 minutes, until shrimp cooks through and outside is crispy.
6. Repeat step 5 to cook remaining shrimp patties.

Quick Shrimp Scampi

Servings: 2

Cooking Time: 5 Minutes

Ingredients:

- 16 to 20 raw large shrimp, peeled, deveined and tails removed
- ½ cup white wine
- freshly ground black pepper
- ¼ cup + 1 tablespoon butter, divided
- 1 clove garlic, sliced
- 1 teaspoon olive oil
- salt, to taste
- juice of ½ lemon, to taste
- ¼ cup chopped fresh parsley

Directions:

1. Start by marinating the shrimp in the white wine and freshly ground black pepper for at least 30 minutes, or as long as 2 hours in the refrigerator.
2. Preheat the toaster oven to 400°F.
3. Melt ¼ cup of butter in a small saucepan on the stovetop. Add the garlic and let the butter simmer, but be sure to not let it burn.
4. Pour the shrimp and marinade into the air fryer oven, letting the marinade drain through to the bottom drawer. Drizzle the olive oil on the shrimp and season well with salt. Air-fry at 400°F for 3 minutes. Turn the shrimp over and pour the garlic butter over the shrimp. Air-fry for another 2 minutes.
5. Remove the shrimp from the air fryer oven and transfer them to a bowl. Squeeze lemon juice over all the shrimp and toss with the chopped parsley and remaining tablespoon of butter. Season to taste with salt and serve immediately.

Stuffed Baked Red Snapper

Servings: 2

Cooking Time: 30 Minutes

Ingredients:
- Stuffing mixture:
- 12 medium shrimp, cooked, peeled, and chopped
- 2 tablespoons multigrain bread crumbs
- 1 teaspoon anchovy paste
- ¼ teaspoon paprika
- Salt to taste
- 2 6-ounce red snapper fillets
- 1 egg
- ½ cup fat-free half-and-half
- 2 tablespoons cooking sherry

Directions:
1. Preheat the toaster oven to 350° F.
2. Combine all the stuffing mixture ingredients in a medium bowl and place a mound of mixture on one end of each fillet. Fold over the other fillet end, skewering the edge with toothpicks.
3. Place the rolled fillets in an oiled or nonstick 8½ × 8½ × 2-inch square baking (cake) pan.
4. Whisk the egg in a small bowl until light in color, then whisk in the half-and-half and sherry. Pour over the fillets. Cover the pan with aluminum foil.
5. BAKE for 30 minutes.

Shrimp Po'boy With Remoulade Sauce

Servings: 6

Cooking Time: 8 Minutes

Ingredients:

- ½ cup all-purpose flour
- ½ teaspoon paprika
- 1 teaspoon garlic powder
- ½ teaspoon black pepper
- ¼ teaspoon salt
- 2 eggs, whisked
- 1½ cups panko breadcrumbs
- 1 pound small shrimp, peeled and deveined
- Six 6-inch French rolls
- 2 cups shredded lettuce
- 12 ⅛-inch tomato slices
- ¾ cup Remoulade Sauce (see the following recipe)

Directions:

1. Preheat the toaster oven to 360°F.
2. In a medium bowl, mix the flour, paprika, garlic powder, pepper, and salt.
3. In a shallow dish, place the eggs.
4. In a third dish, place the panko breadcrumbs.
5. Covering the shrimp in the flour, dip them into the egg, and coat them with the breadcrumbs. Repeat until all shrimp are covered in the breading.
6. Liberally spray the metal trivet that fits inside the air fryer oven with olive oil spray. Place the shrimp onto the trivet, leaving space between the shrimp to flip. Air-fry for 4 minutes, flip the shrimp, and cook another 4 minutes. Repeat until all the shrimp are cooked.
7. Slice the rolls in half. Stuff each roll with shredded lettuce, tomato slices, breaded shrimp, and remoulade sauce. Serve immediately.

Popcorn Crawfish

Servings: 4

Cooking Time: 18 Minutes

Ingredients:
- ½ cup flour, plus 2 tablespoons
- ½ teaspoon garlic powder
- 1½ teaspoons Old Bay Seasoning
- ½ teaspoon onion powder
- ½ cup beer, plus 2 tablespoons
- 12-ounce package frozen crawfish tail meat, thawed and drained
- oil for misting or cooking spray
- Coating
- 1½ cups panko crumbs
- 1 teaspoon Old Bay Seasoning
- ½ teaspoon ground black pepper

Directions:

1. In a large bowl, mix together the flour, garlic powder, Old Bay Seasoning, and onion powder. Stir in beer to blend.
2. Add crawfish meat to batter and stir to coat.
3. Combine the coating ingredients in food processor and pulse to finely crush the crumbs. Transfer crumbs to shallow dish.
4. Preheat the toaster oven to 390°F.
5. Pour the crawfish and batter into a colander to drain. Stir with a spoon to drain excess batter.
6. Working with a handful of crawfish at a time, roll in crumbs and place on a cookie sheet. It's okay if some of the smaller pieces of crawfish meat stick together.
7. Spray breaded crawfish with oil or cooking spray and place all at once into air fryer oven.
8. Air-fry at 390°F for 5 minutes. Stir and mist again with olive oil or spray. Cook 5 more minutes, stir again, and mist lightly again. Continue cooking 5 more minutes, until browned and crispy.

Tasty Fillets With Poblano Sauce

Servings: 2

Cooking Time: 20 Minutes

Ingredients:
- 4 5-ounce thin fish fillets—perch, scrod, catfish, or flounder
- 1 tablespoon olive oil
- Poblano sauce:
- 1 poblano chili, seeded and chopped
- 1 bell pepper, seeded and chopped
- 2 tablespoons chopped onion
- 5 garlic cloves, peeled
- 1 tablespoon flour
- 1 cup fat-free half-and-half
- Salt to taste

Directions:
1. Preheat the toaster oven to 350° F.
2. Brush the fillets with olive oil and transfer to an oiled or nonstick 8½ × 8½ × 2-inch square baking (cake) pan. Set aside.
3. Combine the poblano sauce ingredients and process in a blender or food processor until smooth. Spoon the poblano sauce over the fillets, covering them well.
4. BAKE, uncovered, for 20 minutes, or until the fish flakes easily with a fork.

Shrimp, Chorizo And Fingerling Potatoes

Servings: 4

Cooking Time: 16 Minutes

Ingredients:
- ½ red onion, chopped into 1-inch chunks
- 8 fingerling potatoes, sliced into 1-inch slices or halved lengthwise
- 1 teaspoon olive oil
- salt and freshly ground black pepper
- 8 ounces raw chorizo sausage, sliced into 1-inch chunks
- 16 raw large shrimp, peeled, deveined and tails removed
- 1 lime
- ¼ cup chopped fresh cilantro
- chopped orange zest (optional)

Directions:
1. Preheat the toaster oven to 380°F.
2. Combine the red onion and potato chunks in a bowl and toss with the olive oil, salt and freshly ground black pepper.
3. Transfer the vegetables to the air fryer oven and air-fry for 6 minutes.
4. Add the chorizo chunks and continue to air-fry for another 5 minutes.
5. Add the shrimp, season with salt and continue to air-fry for another 5 minutes.
6. Transfer the tossed shrimp, chorizo and potato to a bowl and squeeze some lime juice over the top to taste. Toss in the fresh cilantro, orange zest and a drizzle of olive oil, and season again to taste.
7. Serve with a fresh green salad.

SNACKS APPETIZERS AND SIDES

Ham And Cheese Palmiers

Servings: 30

Cooking Time: 60 Minutes

Ingredients:

- 1 (9½ by 9-inch) sheet puff pastry, thawed
- 2 tablespoons Dijon mustard
- 2 teaspoons minced fresh thyme
- 2 ounces Parmesan cheese, grated (1 cup)
- 4 ounces thinly sliced deli ham

Directions:

1. Roll puff pastry into 12-inch square on lightly floured counter. Brush evenly with mustard; sprinkle with thyme and Parmesan; pressing gently to adhere, and lay ham evenly over top. Roll up opposite sides of pastry until they meet in middle. Wrap pastry log in plastic wrap and refrigerate until firm, about 1 hour.
2. Adjust toaster oven rack to middle position, select air-fry or convection setting, and preheat the toaster oven to 400 degrees. Line large and small rimmed baking sheets with parchment paper. Using sharp knife, trim ends of log, then slice into ⅓-inch-thick pieces. Space desired number of palmiers at least 1 inch apart on prepared small sheet; space remaining palmiers evenly on prepared large sheet. Re-shape palmiers as needed.
3. Bake small sheet of palmiers until golden brown and crisp, 15 to 25 minutes. Transfer palmiers to wire rack and let cool for 15 minutes before serving. (Palmiers can be held at room temperature for up to 6 hours before serving.)
4. Freeze remaining large sheet of palmiers until firm, about 1 hour. Transfer palmiers to 1-gallon zipper-lock bag and freeze for up to 1 month. Cook frozen palmiers as directed; do not thaw.

Panko-breaded Onion Rings

Servings: 4

Cooking Time: 12 Minutes

Ingredients:

- 1 large sweet onion, cut into ½-inch slices and rings separated
- 2 cups ice water
- ½ cup all-purpose flour
- 1 teaspoon paprika
- 1 teaspoon salt
- ½ teaspoon black pepper
- ½ teaspoon garlic powder
- ¼ teaspoon onion powder
- 1 egg, whisked
- 2 tablespoons milk
- 1 cup breadcrumbs

Directions:

1. Preheat the toaster oven to 400°F.
2. In a large bowl, soak the onion rings in the water for 5 minutes. Drain and pat dry with a towel.
3. In a medium bowl, place the flour, paprika, salt, pepper, garlic powder, and onion powder.
4. In a second bowl, whisk together the egg and milk.
5. In a third bowl, place the breadcrumbs.
6. To bread the onion rings, dip them first into the flour mixture, then into the egg mixture (shaking off the excess), and then into the breadcrumbs. Place the coated onion rings onto a plate while you bread all the rings.
7. Place the onion rings into the air fryer oven in a single layer, sometimes nesting smaller rings into larger rings. Spray with cooking spray. Air-fry for 3 minutes, turn the rings over, and spray with more cooking spray. Air-fry for another 3 to 5 minutes. Cook the rings in batches; you may need to do 2 or 3 batches, depending on the size of your air fryer oven.

Cauliflower-crust Pizza

Servings: 3　　　　　　　　　　　　　　Cooking Time: 14 Minutes

Ingredients:

- 1 pound 2 ounces Riced cauliflower
- 1 plus 1 large egg yolk Large egg(s)
- 3 tablespoons (a little more than ½ ounce) Finely grated Parmesan cheese
- 1½ tablespoons Potato starch
- ¾ teaspoon Dried oregano
- ¾ teaspoon Table salt
- Vegetable oil spray
- 3 tablespoons Purchased pizza sauce
- 6 tablespoons (about 1½ ounces) Shredded semi-firm mozzarella

Directions:

1. Pour the riced cauliflower into a medium microwave-safe bowl. Microwave on high for 4 minutes. Stir well, then cool for 15 minutes.
2. Preheat the toaster oven to 400°F.
3. Pour the riced cauliflower into a clean kitchen towel or a large piece of cheesecloth. Gather the towel or cheesecloth together. Working over the sink, squeeze the moisture out of the cauliflower, getting out as much of the liquid as you can.
4. Pour the squeezed cauliflower back into that same medium bowl and stir in the egg, egg yolk (if using), cheese, potato starch, oregano, and salt to form a loose, uniform "dough."
5. Cut a piece of aluminum foil or parchment paper into a 6-inch circle for a small pizza, a 7-inch circle for a medium one, or an 8-inch circle for a large one. Coat the circle with vegetable oil spray, then place it in the air-fryer oven. Using a small offset spatula or the back of a flatware tablespoon, spread and smooth the cauliflower mixture onto the circle right to the edges. Air-fry undisturbed for 10 minutes.
6. Remove the pan from the air fryer oven. Reduce the machine's temperature to 350°F.
7. Using a large nonstick-safe spatula, flip over the cauliflower circle along with its foil or parchment paper right in the air fryer oven. Peel off and discard the foil or parchment paper. Spread the pizza sauce evenly over the crust and sprinkle with the cheese.
8. Air-fry undisturbed for 4 minutes, or until the cheese has melted and begun to bubble. Remove the pan from the machine and cool for 5 minutes. Use the same spatula to transfer the pizza to a wire rack to cool for 5 minutes more before cutting the pie into wedges to serve.

Shrimp Pirogues

Servings: 8

Cooking Time: 5 Minutes

Ingredients:

- 12 ounces small, peeled, and deveined raw shrimp
- 3 ounces cream cheese, room temperature
- 2 tablespoons plain yogurt
- 1 teaspoon lemon juice
- 1 teaspoon dried dill weed, crushed
- salt
- 4 small hothouse cucumbers, each approximately 6 inches long

Directions:

1. Pour 4 tablespoons water in bottom of air fryer oven.
2. Place shrimp in air fryer oven in single layer and air-fry at 390°F for 5 minutes, just until done. Watch carefully because shrimp cooks quickly, and overcooking makes it tough.
3. Chop shrimp into small pieces, no larger than ½ inch. Refrigerate while mixing the remaining ingredients.
4. With a fork, mash and whip the cream cheese until smooth.
5. Stir in the yogurt and beat until smooth. Stir in lemon juice, dill weed, and chopped shrimp.
6. Taste for seasoning. If needed, add ¼ to ½ teaspoon salt to suit your taste.
7. Store in refrigerator until serving time.
8. When ready to serve, wash and dry cucumbers and split them lengthwise. Scoop out the seeds and turn cucumbers upside down on paper towels to drain for 10 minutes.
9. Just before filling, wipe centers of cucumbers dry. Spoon the shrimp mixture into the pirogues and cut in half crosswise. Serve immediately.

Crispy Tofu Bites

Servings: 4

Cooking Time: 20 Minutes

Ingredients:
- 1 pound Extra firm unflavored tofu
- Vegetable oil spray

Directions:
1. Wrap the piece of tofu in a triple layer of paper towels. Place it on a wooden cutting board and set a large pot on top of it to press out excess moisture. Set aside for 10 minutes.
2. Preheat the toaster oven to 400°F.
3. Remove the pot and unwrap the tofu. Cut it into 1-inch cubes. Place these in a bowl and coat them generously with vegetable oil spray. Toss gently, then spray generously again before tossing, until all are glistening.
4. Gently pour the tofu pieces into the air fryer oven, spread them into as close to one layer as possible, and air-fry for 20 minutes, using kitchen tongs to gently rearrange the pieces at the 7- and 14-minute marks, until light brown and crisp.
5. Gently pour the tofu pieces onto a wire rack. Cool for 5 minutes before serving warm.

Middle Eastern Phyllo Rolls

Servings: 6

Cooking Time: 5 Minutes

Ingredients:

- 6 ounces Lean ground beef or ground lamb
- 3 tablespoons Sliced almonds
- 1 tablespoon Chutney (any variety), finely chopped
- ¼ teaspoon Ground cinnamon
- ¼ teaspoon Ground coriander
- ¼ teaspoon Ground cumin
- ¼ teaspoon Ground dried turmeric
- ¼ teaspoon Table salt
- ¼ teaspoon Ground black pepper
- 6 18 × 14-inch phyllo sheets (thawed, if necessary)
- Olive oil spray

Directions:

1. Set a medium skillet over medium heat for a minute or two, then crumble in the ground meat. Air-fry for 3 minutes, stirring often, or until well browned. Stir in the almonds, chutney, cinnamon, coriander, cumin, turmeric, salt, and pepper until well combined. Remove from the heat, scrape the cooked ground meat mixture into a bowl, and cool for 15 minutes.
2. Preheat the toaster oven to 400°F.
3. Place one sheet of phyllo dough on a clean, dry work surface. (Keep the others covered.) Lightly coat it with olive oil spray, then fold it in half by bringing the short ends together. Place about 3 tablespoons of the ground meat mixture along one of the longer edges, then fold both of the shorter sides of the dough up and over the meat to partially enclose it (and become a border along the sheet of dough). Roll the dough closed, coat it with olive oil spray on all sides, and set it aside seam side down. Repeat this filling and spraying process with the remaining phyllo sheets.
4. Set the rolls seam side down in the air fryer oven in one layer with some air space between them. Air-fry undisturbed for 5 minutes, or until very crisp and golden brown.
5. Use kitchen tongs to transfer the rolls to a wire rack. Cool for only 2 or 3 minutes before serving hot.

Baked Spinach + Artichoke Dip

Servings: 5

Cooking Time: 40 Minutes

Ingredients:
- Nonstick cooking spray
- 2 tablespoons unsalted butter
- ½ medium onion, chopped
- 2 cloves garlic, minced
- 5 ounces frozen, chopped loose-pack spinach (about 1 ¾ cups), thawed and squeezed dry
- 1 (13.75-ounce) can quartered artichoke hearts, drained and chopped
- 1 (8-ounce) package cream cheese, cut into cubes and softened
- ½ cup mayonnaise
- Kosher salt and freshly ground black pepper
- 2 cups shredded Colby Jack or Mexican blend cheese
- ¾ cup shredded Parmesan cheese
- Tortilla chips, pita bread triangles, carrot or celery sticks, broccoli or cauliflower florets, for dipping

Directions:

1. Preheat the toaster oven to 350°F. Spray a 2-quart casserole dish with nonstick cooking spray.

2. Melt the butter in a large skillet over medium-high heat. Add the onion and cook, stirring frequently, until tender, 3 to 5 minutes. Add the garlic and cook, stirring frequently, for 30 seconds. Remove from the heat.

3. Stir in the spinach, artichokes, cream cheese, and mayonnaise. Season with salt and pepper. Blend in the Colby Jack and Parmesan cheeses. Spoon the mixture into the prepared casserole dish. Cover and bake for 20 minutes. Stir the dip and bake, covered, for an additional 10 to 15 minutes, or until hot and melted. Serve with any of the dipping choices.

Wonton Cups

Servings: 6

Cooking Time: 10 Minutes

Ingredients:

- 6 wonton wrappers (3-inch squares)
- 2 Tablespoons melted butter
- Filling of choice

Directions:

1. Preheat toaster oven to 350°F.
2. Carefully press and fold one wonton wrapper in each cup of a 6-cup muffin pan.
3. Very lightly brush edges of wrappers with butter.
4. Bake 8 to 10 minutes or until golden brown.

Crab Rangoon

Servings: 18

Cooking Time: 6 Minutes

Ingredients:

- 4½ tablespoons (a little more than ¼ pound) Crabmeat, preferably backfin or claw, picked over for shells and cartilage
- 1½ ounces (3 tablespoons) Regular or low-fat cream cheese (not fat-free), softened to room temperature
- 1½ tablespoons Minced scallion
- 1½ teaspoons Minced garlic
- 1½ teaspoons Worcestershire sauce
- 18 Wonton wrappers (thawed, if necessary)
- Vegetable oil spray

Directions:

1. Preheat the toaster oven to 400°F.
2. Gently stir the crab, cream cheese, scallion, garlic, and Worcestershire sauce in a medium bowl until well combined.
3. Set a bowl of water on a clean, dry work surface or next to a large cutting board. Set one wonton wrapper on the surface, then put a teaspoonful of the crab mixture in the center of the wrapper. Dip your clean finger in the water and run it around the edge of the wrapper. Bring all four sides up to the center and over the filling, and pinch them together in the middle to seal without covering all of the filling. The traditional look is for the corners of the filled wonton to become four open "flower petals" radiating out from the filled center. Set the filled wonton aside and continue making more as needed. (If you want a video tutorial on filling these, see ours at our YouTube channel, Cooking with Bruce and Mark.)
4. Generously coat the filled wontons with vegetable oil spray. Set them sealed side up in the air fryer oven with a little room among them. Air-fry undisturbed for 6 minutes, or until golden brown and crisp.
5. Use a nonstick-safe spatula to gently transfer the wontons to a wire rack. Cool for 5 minutes before serving warm.

Harissa Roasted Carrots

Servings: 3

Cooking Time: 25 Minutes

Ingredients:
- 1 tablespoon harissa
- 1 tablespoon honey
- 1 tablespoon olive oil
- ¼ teaspoon salt
- 5 large carrots, sliced in half lengthwise
- Chopped parsley, for garnish
- Pomegranate seeds, for garnish
- Chopped toasted walnuts, for garnish

Directions:
1. Combine the harissa, honey, olive oil, and salt in a bowl and whisk together.
2. Select the Preheat function on the Cosori Smart Air Fryer Toaster Oven and press Start/Pause.
3. Line the food tray with foil and place carrots on the tray. Pour the harissa mixture over the carrots and toss to evenly coat.
4. Insert the food tray at mid position in the preheated oven.
5. Select the Bake function, adjust time to 25 minutes, and press Start/Pause.
6. Remove when carrots are golden and tender.
7. Place carrots on a serving platter and garnish with chopped parsley, pomegranate seeds, and walnuts.

Caramelized Onion Dip

Servings: 2

Cooking Time: 20 Minutes

Ingredients:
- 1 tablespoon unsalted butter
- 1 tablespoon olive oil
- 1 large sweet onion, quartered and very thinly sliced crosswise
- Kosher salt
- 1 clove garlic, minced
- 3 tablespoons dry white wine
- ½ teaspoon dried thyme leaves
- ½ teaspoon freshly ground black pepper
- 1 baguette, thinly sliced
- Nonstick cooking spray
- 1 cup shredded Gruyère or Swiss cheese
- ½ cup sour cream
- ½ cup mayonnaise
- ¼ cup shredded Parmesan cheese
- 3 strips bacon, cooked until crisp and crumbled

Directions:
1. Melt the butter and olive oil in a large skillet over medium heat. Add the onion and season with salt. Cook, stirring frequently, for 3 minutes. Reduce the heat to low and cook, stirring occasionally, for 20 to 25 minutes, or until the onions are a deep golden brown color.
2. Increase the heat to medium. Stir in the garlic, wine, thyme, and pepper. Cook, stirring frequently, for 3 minutes or until the wine has mostly evaporated. Remove from the heat.
3. Meanwhile, toast the baguette slices in the toaster oven until golden brown and crisp; set aside.
4. Preheat the toaster oven to 350°F. Spray a 1-quart casserole with nonstick cooking spray.
5. Stir the Gruyère, sour cream, mayonnaise, Parmesan, and bacon into the onions. Spoon the mixture into the prepared casserole dish. Cover and bake for 20 minutes or until hot and the cheese is melted. Allow to stand for 5 to 10 minutes before serving. To serve, spoon the warm onion-cheese mixture onto the toast.

Corn Dog Muffins

Servings: 8

Cooking Time: 10 Minutes

Ingredients:
- 1¼ cups sliced kosher hotdogs (3 or 4, depending on size)
- ½ cup flour
- ½ cup yellow cornmeal
- 2 teaspoons baking powder
- ½ cup skim milk
- 1 egg
- 2 tablespoons canola oil
- 8 foil muffin cups, paper liners removed
- cooking spray
- mustard or your favorite dipping sauce

Directions:
1. Slice each hot dog in half lengthwise, then cut in ¼-inch half-moon slices. Set aside.
2. Preheat the toaster oven to 390°F.
3. In a large bowl, stir together flour, cornmeal, and baking powder.
4. In a small bowl, beat together the milk, egg, and oil until just blended.
5. Pour egg mixture into dry ingredients and stir with a spoon to mix well.
6. Stir in sliced hot dogs.
7. Spray the foil cups lightly with cooking spray.
8. Divide mixture evenly into muffin cups.
9. Place 4 muffin cups in the air fryer oven and air-fry for 5 minutes.
10. Reduce temperature to 360°F and cook 5 minutes or until toothpick inserted in center of muffin comes out clean.
11. Repeat steps 9 and 10 to bake remaining corn dog muffins.
12. Serve with mustard or other sauces for dipping.

Bacon Bites

Servings: 6

Cooking Time: 20 Minutes

Ingredients:

- ½ cup packed dark brown sugar
- 6 slices bacon
- 6 very thin breadsticks from a 3-ounce package

Directions:

1. Preheat the toaster oven to 350°F. Line a 12 x 12-inch baking pan with aluminum foil.
2. Spread the brown sugar on a large plate. Wrap a bacon slice around each breadstick. Roll the bacon-wrapped breadstick in the brown sugar and press to adhere to the bacon. Place on the prepared pan.
3. Bake for 18 to 20 minutes, or until the bacon is cooked through. Immediately remove and place the warm sticks on wax paper (to prevent sticking). Let cool to room temperature before serving.

POULTRY

Tasty Meat Loaf

Servings: 4
Cooking Time: 35 Minutes

Ingredients:
- 1 to 1½ pounds ground turkey or chicken breast
- 1 egg
- 1 tablespoon chopped fresh parsley
- 2 tablespoons chopped bell pepper
- 3 tablespoons chopped canned mushrooms
- 2 tablespoons chopped onion
- 2 garlic cloves, minced
- ½ cup multigrain bread crumbs
- 1 tablespoon Worcestershire sauce
- 1 tablespoon ketchup
- Freshly ground black pepper to taste

Directions:
1. Preheat the toaster oven to 400° F.
2. Combine all the ingredients in a large bowl and press into a regular-size 4½ × 8½ × 2¼-inch loaf pan.
3. BAKE for 35 minutes, or until browned on top.

Fiesta Chicken Plate

Servings: 4

Cooking Time: 15 Minutes

Ingredients:
- 1 pound boneless, skinless chicken breasts (2 large breasts)
- 2 tablespoons lime juice
- 1 teaspoon cumin
- ½ teaspoon salt
- ½ cup grated Pepper Jack cheese
- 1 16-ounce can refried beans
- ½ cup salsa
- 2 cups shredded lettuce
- 1 medium tomato, chopped
- 2 avocados, peeled and sliced
- 1 small onion, sliced into thin rings
- sour cream
- tortilla chips (optional)

Directions:
1. Split each chicken breast in half lengthwise.
2. Mix lime juice, cumin, and salt together and brush on all surfaces of chicken breasts.
3. Place in air fryer oven and air-fry at 390°F for 15 minutes, until well done.
4. Divide the cheese evenly over chicken breasts and air-fry for an additional minute to melt cheese.
5. While chicken is cooking, heat refried beans on stovetop or in microwave.
6. When ready to serve, divide beans among 4 plates. Place chicken breasts on top of beans and spoon salsa over. Arrange the lettuce, tomatoes, and avocados artfully on each plate and scatter with the onion rings.
7. Pass sour cream at the table and serve with tortilla chips if desired.

Tender Chicken Meatballs

Servings: 4

Cooking Time: 30 Minutes

Ingredients:
- 1 pound lean ground chicken
- ½ cup bread crumbs
- 1 large egg
- 1 scallion, both white and green parts, finely chopped
- ¼ cup whole milk
- ¼ cup shredded, unsweetened coconut
- 1 tablespoon low-sodium soy sauce
- 1 teaspoon minced garlic
- 1 teaspoon fresh ginger, peeled and grated
- Pinch cayenne powder
- Oil spray (hand-pumped)

Directions:
1. Preheat the toaster oven to 375°F on BAKE for 5 minutes.
2. Line the baking tray with parchment and set aside.
3. In a large bowl, mix the chicken, bread crumbs, egg, scallion, milk, coconut, soy sauce, garlic, ginger, and cayenne until very well combined.
4. Shape the chicken mixture into 1½-inch balls and place them in a single layer on the baking tray. Do not overcrowd them.
5. In position 2, bake for 20 minutes, turning halfway through, until they are cooked through and evenly browned. Serve.

Guiltless Bacon

Servings: 4

Cooking Time: 10 Minutes

Ingredients:

- 6 slices lean turkey bacon, placed on a broiling pan

Directions:

1. BROIL 5 minutes, turn the pieces, and broil again for 5 more minutes, or until done to your preference. Press the slices between paper towels and serve immediately.

Fried Chicken

Servings: 4   Cooking Time: 40 Minutes

Ingredients:

- 12 skin-on chicken drumsticks
- 1 cup buttermilk
- 1½ cups all-purpose flour
- 1 tablespoon smoked paprika
- ¾ teaspoon celery salt
- ¾ teaspoon dried mustard
- ½ teaspoon garlic powder
- ½ teaspoon freshly ground black pepper
- ½ teaspoon sea salt
- ½ teaspoon dried thyme
- ¼ teaspoon dried oregano
- 4 large eggs
- Oil spray (hand-pumped)

Directions:

1. Place the chicken and buttermilk in a medium bowl, cover, and refrigerate for at least 1 hour, up to overnight.
2. Preheat the toaster oven to 375°F on AIR FRY for 5 minutes.
3. In a large bowl, stir the flour, paprika, celery salt, mustard, garlic powder, pepper, salt, thyme, and oregano until well mixed.
4. Beat the eggs until frothy in a medium bowl and set them beside the flour.
5. Place the air-fryer basket in the baking tray and generously spray it with the oil.
6. Dredge a chicken drumstick in the flour, then the eggs, and then in the flour again, thickly coating it, and place the drumstick in the basket. Repeat with 5 more drumsticks and spray them all lightly with the oil on all sides.
7. In position 2, air fry for 20 minutes, turning halfway through, until golden brown and crispy with an internal temperature of 165°F.
8. Repeat with the remaining chicken, covering the cooked chicken loosely with foil to keep it warm. Serve.

Crispy Fried Onion Chicken Breasts

Servings: 2

Cooking Time: 13 Minutes

Ingredients:
- ¼ cup all-purpose flour
- salt and freshly ground black pepper
- 1 egg
- 2 tablespoons Dijon mustard
- 1½ cups crispy fried onions (like French's®)
- ½ teaspoon paprika
- 2 (5-ounce) boneless, skinless chicken breasts
- vegetable or olive oil, in a spray bottle

Directions:
1. Preheat the toaster oven to 380°F.
2. Set up a dredging station with three shallow dishes. Place the flour in the first shallow dish and season well with salt and freshly ground black pepper. Combine the egg and Dijon mustard in a second shallow dish and whisk until smooth. Place the fried onions in a sealed bag and using a rolling pin, crush them into coarse crumbs. Combine these crumbs with the paprika in the third shallow dish.
3. Dredge the chicken breasts in the flour. Shake off any excess flour and dip them into the egg mixture. Let any excess egg drip off. Then coat both sides of the chicken breasts with the crispy onions. Press the crumbs onto the chicken breasts with your hands to make sure they are well adhered.
4. Spray or brush the bottom of the air fryer oven with oil. Transfer the chicken breasts to the air fryer oven and air-fry at 380°F for 13 minutes, turning the chicken over halfway through the cooking time.
5. Serve immediately.

Chicken Schnitzel Dogs

Servings: 4

Cooking Time: 10 Minutes

Ingredients:
- ½ cup flour
- ½ teaspoon salt
- 1 teaspoon marjoram
- 1 teaspoon dried parsley flakes
- ½ teaspoon thyme
- 1 egg
- 1 teaspoon lemon juice
- 1 teaspoon water
- 1 cup breadcrumbs
- 4 chicken tenders, pounded thin
- oil for misting or cooking spray
- 4 whole-grain hotdog buns
- 4 slices Gouda cheese
- 1 small Granny Smith apple, thinly sliced
- ½ cup shredded Napa cabbage
- coleslaw dressing

Directions:
1. In a shallow dish, mix together the flour, salt, marjoram, parsley, and thyme.
2. In another shallow dish, beat together egg, lemon juice, and water.
3. Place breadcrumbs in a third shallow dish.
4. Cut each of the flattened chicken tenders in half lengthwise.
5. Dip flattened chicken strips in flour mixture, then egg wash. Let excess egg drip off and roll in breadcrumbs. Spray both sides with oil or cooking spray.
6. Air-fry at 390°F for 5 minutes. Spray with oil, turn over, and spray other side.
7. Air-fry for 3 to 5 minutes more, until well done and crispy brown.
8. To serve, place 2 schnitzel strips on bottom of each hot dog bun. Top with cheese, sliced apple, and cabbage. Drizzle with coleslaw dressing and top with other half of bun.

Pecan Turkey Cutlets

Servings: 4

Cooking Time: 12 Minutes

Ingredients:

- ¾ cup panko breadcrumbs
- ¼ teaspoon salt
- ¼ teaspoon pepper
- ¼ teaspoon dry mustard
- ¼ teaspoon poultry seasoning
- ½ cup pecans
- ¼ cup cornstarch
- 1 egg, beaten
- 1 pound turkey cutlets, ½-inch thick
- salt and pepper
- oil for misting or cooking spray

Directions:

1. Place the panko crumbs, ¼ teaspoon salt, ¼ teaspoon pepper, mustard, and poultry seasoning in food processor. Process until crumbs are finely crushed. Add pecans and process in short pulses just until nuts are finely chopped. Go easy so you don't overdo it!
2. Preheat the toaster oven to 360°F.
3. Place cornstarch in one shallow dish and beaten egg in another. Transfer coating mixture from food processor into a third shallow dish.
4. Sprinkle turkey cutlets with salt and pepper to taste.
5. Dip cutlets in cornstarch and shake off excess. Then dip in beaten egg and roll in crumbs, pressing to coat well. Spray both sides with oil or cooking spray.
6. Place 2 cutlets in air fryer oven in a single layer and air-fry for 12 minutes or until juices run clear.
7. Repeat step 6 to cook remaining cutlets.

Chicken Potpie

Servings: 4
Cooking Time: 48 Minutes

Ingredients:
- Pie filling:
- 1 tablespoon unbleached flour
- ½ cup evaporated skim milk
- 4 skinless, boneless chicken thighs, cut into 1-inch cubes
- 1 cup potatoes, peeled and cut into ½-inch pieces
- ½ cup frozen green peas
- ½ cup thinly sliced carrot
- 2 tablespoons chopped onion
- ½ cup chopped celery
- 1 teaspoon garlic powder
- Salt and freshly ground black pepper to taste
- 8 sheets phyllo pastry, thawed Olive oil

Directions:
1. Preheat the toaster oven to 400° F.
2. Whisk the flour into the milk until smooth in a 1-quart 8½ × 8½ × 4-inch ovenproof baking dish. Add the remaining filling ingredients and mix well. Adjust the seasonings to taste. Cover the dish with aluminum foil.
3. BAKE for 40 minutes, or until the carrot, potatoes, and celery are tender. Remove from the oven and uncover.
4. Place one sheet of phyllo pastry on top of the baked pie-filling mixture, bending the edges to fit the shape of the baking dish. Brush the sheet with olive oil. Add another sheet on top of it and brush with oil. Continue adding the remaining sheets, brushing each one, until the crust is completed. Brush the top with oil.
5. BAKE for 6 minutes, or until the phyllo pastry is browned.

Italian Baked Chicken

Servings: 4

Cooking Time: 28 Minutes

Ingredients:
- 1 pound boneless, skinless chicken breasts
- ½ cup dry white wine
- 3 tablespoons olive oil
- 2 tablespoons white wine vinegar
- 2 tablespoons fresh lemon juice
- 2 teaspoons Italian seasoning
- 3 cloves garlic, minced
- ½ teaspoon kosher salt
- ¼ teaspoon freshly ground black pepper
- 4 slices salami, cut in half
- 3 tablespoons shredded Parmesan cheese

Directions:

1. If the chicken breasts are large and thick, slice each breast in half lengthwise. Place the chicken in a shallow baking dish.

2. Combine the white wine, olive oil, vinegar, lemon juice, Italian seasoning, garlic, salt, and pepper in a small bowl. Pour over the chicken breasts. Cover and refrigerate for 2 to 8 hours, turning the chicken occasionally to coat.

3. Preheat the toaster oven to 375 ºF.

4. Drain the chicken, discarding the marinade, and place the chicken in an ungreased 12 x 12-inch baking pan. Bake, uncovered, for 20 to 25 minutes or until the chicken is done and a meat thermometer registers 165 ºF. Place one slice salami (two pieces) on top of each piece of the chicken. Sprinkle the Parmesan evenly over the chicken breasts and broil for 2 to 3 minutes, or until the cheese is melted and starting to brown.

Tandoori Chicken Legs

Servings: 2

Cooking Time: 30 Minutes

Ingredients:

- 1 cup plain yogurt
- 2 cloves garlic, minced
- 1 tablespoon grated fresh ginger
- 2 teaspoons paprika
- 2 teaspoons ground coriander
- 1 teaspoon ground turmeric
- 1 teaspoon salt
- ¼ teaspoon ground cayenne pepper
- juice of 1 lime
- 2 bone-in, skin-on chicken legs
- fresh cilantro leaves

Directions:

1. Make the marinade by combining the yogurt, garlic, ginger, spices and lime juice. Make slashes into the chicken legs to help the marinade penetrate the meat. Pour the marinade over the chicken legs, cover and let the chicken marinate for at least an hour or overnight in the refrigerator.
2. Preheat the toaster oven oven to 380°F.
3. Transfer the chicken legs from the marinade to the air fryer oven, reserving any extra marinade. Air-fry for 15 minutes. Flip the chicken over and pour the remaining marinade over the top. Air-fry for another 15 minutes, watching to make sure it doesn't brown too much. If it does start to get too brown, you can loosely tent the chicken with aluminum foil, tucking the ends of the foil under the chicken to stop it from blowing around.
4. Serve over rice with some fresh cilantro on top.

Chicken Adobo

Servings: 6

Cooking Time: 12 Minutes

Ingredients:

- 6 boneless chicken thighs
- ¼ cup soy sauce or tamari
- ½ cup rice wine vinegar
- 4 cloves garlic, minced
- ⅛ teaspoon crushed red pepper flakes
- ½ teaspoon black pepper

Directions:

1. Place the chicken thighs into a resealable plastic bag with the soy sauce or tamari, the rice wine vinegar, the garlic, and the crushed red pepper flakes. Seal the bag and let the chicken marinate at least 1 hour in the refrigerator.
2. Preheat the toaster oven to 400°F.
3. Drain the chicken and pat dry with a paper towel. Season the chicken with black pepper and liberally spray with cooking spray.
4. Place the chicken in the air fryer oven and air-fry for 9 minutes, turn over at 9 minutes and check for an internal temperature of 165°F, and cook another 3 minutes.

Sesame Chicken Breasts

Servings: 2

Cooking Time: 20 Minutes

Ingredients:
- Mixture:
- 2 tablespoons sesame oil
- 2 teaspoons soy sauce
- 2 teaspoons balsamic vinegar
- 2 skinless, boneless chicken breast filets
- 3 tablespoons sesame seeds

Directions:

1. Combine the mixture ingredients in a small bowl and brush the filets liberally. Reserve the mixture. Place the filets on a broiling rack with a pan underneath.
2. BROIL 15 minutes, or until the meat is tender and the juices, when the meat is pierced, run clear. Remove from the oven and brush the filets with the remaining mixture. Place the sesame seeds on a plate and press the chicken breast halves into the seeds, coating well.
3. BROIL for 5 minutes, or until the sesame seeds are browned.

DESSERTS

Blueberry Cookies

Servings: 4

Cooking Time: 12 Minutes

Ingredients:

- 1 egg
- 1 tablespoon margarine, at room temperature
- ⅓ cup sugar
- 1¼ cups unbleached flour
- Salt to taste
- 1 teaspoon baking powder
- 1 10-ounce package frozen blueberries, well drained, or
- 1½ cups fresh blueberries, rinsed and drained

Directions:

1. Preheat the toaster oven to 400° F.
2. Beat together the egg, margarine, and sugar in a medium bowl with an electric mixer until smooth. Add the flour, salt, and baking powder, mixing thoroughly. Gently stir in the blueberries just to blend. Do not overmix.
3. Drop by teaspoonfuls on an oiled or nonstick 6½ × 10-inch baking sheet or an oiled or nonstick 8½ × 8½ × 2-inch square baking (cake) pan.
4. BAKE for 12 minutes, or until the cookies are golden brown.

Giant Buttery Oatmeal Cookie

Servings: 4   Cooking Time: 16 Minutes

Ingredients:

- 1 cup Rolled oats (not quick-cooking or steel-cut oats)
- ½ cup All-purpose flour
- ½ teaspoon Baking soda
- ½ teaspoon Ground cinnamon
- ½ teaspoon Table salt
- 3½ tablespoons Butter, at room temperature
- ⅓ cup Packed dark brown sugar
- 1½ tablespoons Granulated white sugar
- 3 tablespoons (or 1 medium egg, well beaten) Pasteurized egg substitute, such as Egg Beaters
- ¾ teaspoon Vanilla extract
- ⅓ cup Chopped pecans
- Baking spray

Directions:

1. Preheat the toaster oven to 350°F.
2. Stir the oats, flour, baking soda, cinnamon, and salt in a bowl until well combined.
3. Using an electric hand mixer at medium speed, beat the butter, brown sugar, and granulated white sugar until creamy and thick, about 3 minutes, scraping down the inside of the bowl occasionally. Beat in the egg substitute or egg (as applicable) and vanilla until uniform.
4. Scrape down and remove the beaters. Fold in the flour mixture and pecans with a rubber spatula just until all the flour is moistened and the nuts are even throughout the dough.
5. For a small air fryer oven, coat the inside of a 6-inch round cake pan with baking spray. For a medium air fryer oven, coat the inside of a 7-inch round cake pan with baking spray. And for a large air fryer oven, coat the inside of an 8-inch round cake pan with baking spray. Scrape and gently press the dough into the prepared pan, spreading it into an even layer to the perimeter.
6. Set the pan in the toaster oven and air-fry undisturbed for 16 minutes, or until puffed and browned.
7. Transfer the pan to a wire rack and cool for 10 minutes. Loosen the cookie from the perimeter with a spatula, then invert the pan onto a cutting board and let the cookie come free. Remove the pan and reinvert the cookie onto the wire rack. Cool for 5 minutes more before slicing into wedges to serve.

Pineapple Tartlets

Servings: 4

Cooking Time: 20 Minutes

Ingredients:
- Vegetable oil
- 6 sheets phyllo pastry
- 1 8-ounce can crushed pineapple, drained
- 3 tablespoons low-fat cottage cheese
- 2 tablespoons orange or pineapple marmalade
- 6 teaspoons concentrated thawed frozen orange juice
- Vanilla frozen yogurt or nonfat whipped topping

Directions:

1. Preheat the toaster oven to 350° F.
2. Brush the pans of a 6-muffin tin with vegetable oil. Lay a phyllo sheet on a clean, flat surface and brush with oil. Fold the sheet into quarters to fit the muffin pan. Repeat the process for the remaining phyllo sheets and pans.
3. BAKE for 5 minutes, or until lightly browned. Remove from the oven and cool.
4. Combine the pineapple, cottage cheese, and marmalade in a small bowl, mixing well. Fill the phyllo shells (in the pans) with equal portions of the mixture. Drizzle 1 teaspoon orange juice concentrate over each.
5. BAKE at 400° F. for 15 minutes, or until the filling is cooked. Cool and remove the tartlets carefully from the muffin pans to dessert dishes. Top with vanilla frozen yogurt or nonfat whipped topping.

Baked Apple

Servings: 4

Cooking Time: 20 Minutes

Ingredients:

- 3 small Honey Crisp or other baking apples
- 3 tablespoons maple syrup
- 3 tablespoons chopped pecans
- 1 tablespoon firm butter, cut into 6 pieces

Directions:

1. Put ½ cup water in the drawer of the air fryer oven.
2. Wash apples well and dry them.
3. Split apples in half. Remove core and a little of the flesh to make a cavity for the pecans.
4. Place apple halves in air fryer oven, cut side up.
5. Spoon 1½ teaspoons pecans into each cavity.
6. Spoon ½ tablespoon maple syrup over pecans in each apple.
7. Top each apple with ½ teaspoon butter.
8. Preheat the toaster oven to 360°F and air-fry for 20 minutes, until apples are tender.

Strawberry Blueberry Cobbler

Servings: 6

Cooking Time: 30 Minutes

Ingredients:
- Berry filling:
- 1 10-ounce package frozen blueberries, thawed, or 1½ cups fresh blueberries
- 1 10-ounce package frozen strawberries, thawed, or 1½ cups fresh strawberries
- ½ cup strawberry preserves
- ¼ cup unbleached flour
- 1 teaspoon lemon juice
- Topping:
- ¼ cup unbleached flour
- 2 tablespoons margarine
- 1 tablespoon fat-free half-and-half
- ½ teaspoon baking powder
- 1 tablespoon sugar

Directions:
1. Preheat the toaster oven to 400° F.
2. Combine the berry filling ingredients in a large bowl, mixing well. Transfer to an oiled or nonstick 8½ × 8½ × 2-inch square baking (cake) pan. Set aside.
3. Combine the topping ingredients in a small bowl, blending with a fork until the mixture is crumbly. Sprinkle the mixture evenly over the berries.
4. BAKE for 30 minutes, or until the top is lightly browned.

Maple-glazed Pumpkin Pie

Servings: 2

Cooking Time: 10 Minutes

Ingredients:
- Filling:
- 1 15-ounce can pumpkin pie filling
- 1 12-ounce can low-fat evaporated milk
- 1 egg
- 3 tablespoons maple syrup
- ½ teaspoon grated nutmeg
- ½ teaspoon ground ginger
- 1 teaspoon ground cinnamon
- Salt to taste
- 1 Apple Juice Piecrust, baked (recipe follows)
- Dark glaze:
- 3 tablespoons maple syrup
- 2 tablespoons dark brown sugar

Directions:
1. Preheat the toaster oven to 400° F.
2. Combine all the filling ingredients in a large bowl and beat with an electric mixer until smooth. Pour into the piecrust shell.
3. BAKE for 40 minutes, or until a knife inserted in the center comes out clean.
4. Combine the dark glaze ingredients in a baking pan.
5. BROIL for 5 minutes, or until bubbling. Remove from the oven and stir to dissolve the sugar. Broil again for 3 minutes, or until the liquid is thickened and the sugar is dissolved. Spoon on top of the cooled pumpkin pie, spreading evenly, then chill for at least 1 hour before serving.

Coconut Rice Pudding

Servings: 6

Cooking Time: 55 Minutes

Ingredients:

- ½ cup short-grain brown rice
- Pudding mixture:
- 1 egg, beaten
- 1 tablespoon cornstarch
- ½ cup fat-free half-and-half
- ½ cup chopped raisins
- 1 teaspoon vanilla extract
- ½ teaspoon ground cinnamon
- ½ teaspoon grated nutmeg
- Salt to taste
- ¼ cup shredded sweetened coconut
- Fat-free whipped topping

Directions:

1. Preheat the toaster oven to 400° F.
2. Combine the rice and 1½ cups water in a 1-quart 8½ × 8½ × 4-inch ovenproof baking dish. Cover with aluminum foil.
3. BAKE, covered, for 45 minutes, or until the rice is tender. Remove from the oven and add the pudding mixture ingredients, mixing well.
4. BAKE, uncovered, for 10 minutes, or until the top is lightly browned. Sprinkle the top with coconut and chill before serving. Top with fat-free whipped topping.

Orange-glazed Brownies

Servings: 12

Cooking Time: 30 Minutes

Ingredients:
- 3 squares unsweetened chocolate
- 3 tablespoons margarine
- 1 cup sugar
- ½ cup orange juice
- 2 eggs
- 1½ cups unbleached flour
- 1 teaspoon baking powder
- Salt to taste
- 1 tablespoon grated orange zest
- Orange Glaze (recipe follows)

Directions:

1. BROIL the chocolate and margarine in an oiled or nonstick 8½ × 8½ × 2-inch square baking (cake) pan for 3 minutes, or until almost melted. Remove from the oven and stir until completely melted. Transfer the chocolate/margarine mixture to a medium bowl.
2. Beat in the sugar, orange juice, and eggs with an electric mixer. Stir in the flour, baking powder, salt, and orange zest and mix until well blended. Pour into the oiled or nonstick square cake pan.
3. BAKE at 350° F. for 30 minutes, or until a toothpick inserted in the center comes out clean. Make holes over the entire top by piercing with a fork or toothpick. Paint with Orange Glaze and cut into squares.

Giant Oatmeal–peanut Butter Cookie

Servings: 4

Cooking Time: 18 Minutes

Ingredients:

- 1 cup Rolled oats (not quick-cooking or steel-cut oats)
- ½ cup All-purpose flour
- ½ teaspoon Ground cinnamon
- ½ teaspoon Baking soda
- ⅓ cup Packed light brown sugar
- ¼ cup Solid vegetable shortening
- 2 tablespoons Natural-style creamy peanut butter
- 3 tablespoons Granulated white sugar
- 2 tablespoons (or 1 small egg, well beaten) Pasteurized egg substitute, such as Egg Beaters
- ⅓ cup Roasted, salted peanuts, chopped
- Baking spray

Directions:

1. Preheat the toaster oven to 350°F..
2. Stir the oats, flour, cinnamon, and baking soda in a bowl until well combined.
3. Using an electric hand mixer at medium speed, beat the brown sugar, shortening, peanut butter, granulated white sugar, and egg substitute or egg (as applicable) until smooth and creamy, about 3 minutes, scraping down the inside of the bowl occasionally.
4. Scrape down and remove the beaters. Fold in the flour mixture and peanuts with a rubber spatula just until all the flour is moistened and the peanut bits are evenly distributed in the dough.
5. For a small air fryer oven, coat the inside of a 6-inch round cake pan with baking spray. For a medium air fryer oven, coat the inside of a 7-inch round cake pan with baking spray. And for a large air fryer oven, coat the inside of an 8-inch round cake pan with baking spray. Scrape and gently press the dough into the prepared pan, spreading it into an even layer to the perimeter.
6. Set the pan in the air fryer oven and air-fry undisturbed for 18 minutes, or until well browned.
7. Transfer the pan to a wire rack and cool for 15 minutes. Loosen the cookie from the perimeter with a spatula, then invert the pan onto a cutting board and let the cookie come free. Remove the pan and reinvert the cookie onto the wire rack. Cool for 5 minutes more before slicing into wedges to serve.

Freezer-to-oven Chocolate Chip Cookies

Servings: 6

Cooking Time: 15 Minutes

Ingredients:
- 2 ½ cups all-purpose flour
- 1 teaspoon baking soda
- ½ teaspoon table salt
- ¼ teaspoon baking powder
- 1 cup unsalted butter, softened
- 1 cup packed dark brown sugar
- ¾ cup granulated sugar
- 2 large eggs
- 2 teaspoons pure vanilla extract
- 1 (12-ounce) package semisweet chocolate chips

Directions:
1. Preheat the toaster oven to 375°F. Line a 12 x 12-inch baking sheet with parchment paper.
2. Whisk the flour, baking soda, salt, and baking powder in a medium bowl; set aside.
3. Beat the butter, brown sugar, and granulated sugar in a large bowl with a handheld mixer at medium-high speed for 2 minutes or until creamy. Beat in the eggs, one at a time, beating well after each addition. Beat in the vanilla. Mix in the dry ingredients until blended. Stir in the chocolate chips.
4. Using a 2-tablespoon scoop, shape the batter into balls about 1 ½ inches in diameter. Arrange the cookies 1 inch apart on the prepared baking sheet. Bake for 13 to 15 minutes or until golden brown. Remove from the oven and let cool for 1 minute, then transfer the cookies to a wire rack.

Campfire Banana Boats

Servings: 4

Cooking Time: 20 Minutes

Ingredients:
- 4 medium, unpeeled ripe bananas
- ¼ cup dark chocolate chips
- 4 teaspoons shredded, unsweetened coconut
- ½ cup mini marshmallows
- 4 graham crackers, chopped

Directions:
1. Preheat the toaster oven to 400°F on BAKE for 5 minutes.
2. Cut the bananas lengthwise through the skin about halfway through. Open the pocket to create a space for the other ingredients.
3. Evenly divide the chocolate, coconut, marshmallows, and graham crackers among the bananas.
4. Tear off four 12-inch squares of foil and place the bananas in the center of each. Crimp the foil around the banana to form a boat.
5. Place the bananas on the baking tray, two at a time, and in position 2, bake for 10 minutes until the fillings are gooey and the banana is warmed through.
6. Repeat with the remaining two bananas and serve.

Pear And Almond Biscotti Crumble

Servings: 6

Cooking Time: 65 Minutes

Ingredients:

- 7-inch cake pan or ceramic dish
- 3 pears, peeled, cored and sliced
- ½ cup brown sugar
- ¼ teaspoon ground ginger
- 1 teaspoon ground cinnamon
- ⅛ teaspoon ground nutmeg
- 2 tablespoons cornstarch
- 1¼ cups (4 to 5) almond biscotti, coarsely crushed
- ¼ cup all-purpose flour
- ¼ cup sliced almonds
- ¼ cup butter, melted

Directions:

1. Combine the pears, brown sugar, ginger, cinnamon, nutmeg and cornstarch in a bowl. Toss to combine and then pour the pear mixture into a greased 7-inch cake pan or ceramic dish.
2. Combine the crushed biscotti, flour, almonds and melted butter in a medium bowl. Toss with a fork until the mixture resembles large crumbles. Sprinkle the biscotti crumble over the pears and cover the pan with aluminum foil.
3. Preheat the toaster oven to 350°F.
4. Air-fry at 350°F for 60 minutes. Remove the aluminum foil and air-fry for an additional 5 minutes to brown the crumble layer.
5. Serve warm.

Cinnamon Sugar Rolls

Servings: 8

Cooking Time: 10 Minutes

Ingredients:
- ½ cup margarine
- Filling mixture:
- 1 tablespoon ground cinnamon
- ½ cup brown sugar
- ½ cup finely chopped walnuts
- 10 sheets phyllo pastry, thawed

Directions:

1. BROIL the margarine in an oiled or nonstick 8½ × 8½ × 2-inch square baking (cake) pan for 3 minutes, or until almost melted. Remove from the oven and stir until melted (the pan will be hot and the margarine will continue to melt). Set aside.
2. Combine the filling mixture in a small bowl, mixing well.
3. Lay a sheet of phyllo pastry on a clean flat surface. Brush with the melted margarine, sprinkle with a heaping tablespoon of the filling mixture, and spread evenly to cover the sheet of pastry. Repeat the brushing and sprinkling procedure for each sheet, layering one on top of the other until all 10 sheets are done. Use up any remaining filling mixture on the last sheet. Starting at the 9-inch (long) edge, slowly roll all of the sheets up like a jelly roll. With a sharp knife, cut the roll into 1¼-inch slices. Place the slices on an oiled or nonstick baking sheet or baking pan.
4. BAKE at 350° F. for 10 minutes, or until golden brown.

BEEF PORK AND LAMB

Italian Sausage & Peppers

Servings: 6   Cooking Time: 25 Minutes

Ingredients:

- 1 6-ounce can tomato paste
- ⅔ cup water
- 1 8-ounce can tomato sauce
- 1 teaspoon dried parsley flakes
- ½ teaspoon garlic powder
- ⅛ teaspoon oregano
- ½ pound mild Italian bulk sausage
- 1 tablespoon extra virgin olive oil
- ½ large onion, cut in 1-inch chunks
- 4 ounces fresh mushrooms, sliced
- 1 large green bell pepper, cut in 1-inch chunks
- 8 ounces spaghetti, cooked
- Parmesan cheese for serving

Directions:

1. In a large saucepan or skillet, stir together the tomato paste, water, tomato sauce, parsley, garlic, and oregano. Heat on stovetop over very low heat while preparing meat and vegetables.
2. Break sausage into small chunks, about ½-inch pieces. Place in air fryer oven baking pan.
3. Air-fry at 390°F for 5 minutes. Stir. Cook 7 minutes longer or until sausage is well done. Remove from pan, drain on paper towels, and add to the sauce mixture.
4. If any sausage grease remains in baking pan, pour it off or use paper towels to soak it up. (Be careful handling that hot pan!)
5. Place olive oil, onions, and mushrooms in pan and stir. Air-fry for 5 minutes or just until tender. Using a slotted spoon, transfer onions and mushrooms from baking pan into the sauce and sausage mixture.
6. Place bell pepper chunks in air fryer oven baking pan and air-fry for 8 minutes or until tender. When done, stir into sauce with sausage and other vegetables.
7. Serve over cooked spaghetti with plenty of Parmesan cheese.

Lamb Koftas Meatballs

Servings: 3

Cooking Time: 8 Minutes

Ingredients:
- 1 pound ground lamb
- 1 teaspoon ground cumin
- 1 teaspoon ground coriander
- 2 tablespoons chopped fresh mint
- 1 egg, beaten
- ½ teaspoon salt
- freshly ground black pepper

Directions:
1. Combine all ingredients in a bowl and mix together well. Divide the mixture into 10 portions. Roll each portion into a ball and then by cupping the meatball in your hand, shape it into an oval.
2. Preheat the toaster oven to 400°F.
3. Air-fry the koftas for 8 minutes.
4. Serve warm with the cucumber-yogurt dip.

Cilantro-crusted Flank Steak

Servings: 2
Cooking Time: 16 Minutes

Ingredients:

- Coating:
- 2 tablespoons chopped onion
- 1 tablespoon olive oil
- 2 tablespoons plain nonfat yogurt
- 1 plum tomato
- ½ cup fresh cilantro leaves
- 2 tablespoons cooking sherry
- ¼ teaspoon hot sauce
- 1 teaspoon garlic powder
- ½ teaspoon chili powder
- Salt and freshly ground black pepper
- 2 8-ounce flank steaks

Directions:

1. Process the coating ingredients in a blender or food processor until smooth. Spread half of the coating mixture on top of the flank steaks. Place the steaks on a broiling rack with a pan underneath.
2. BROIL for 8 minutes. Turn with tongs, spread the remaining mixture on the steaks, and broil again for 8 minutes, or until done to your preference.

Crunchy Fried Pork Loin Chops

Servings: 3

Cooking Time: 12 Minutes

Ingredients:
- 1 cup All-purpose flour or tapioca flour
- 1 Large egg(s), well beaten
- 1½ cups Seasoned Italian-style dried bread crumbs (gluten-free, if a concern)
- 3 4- to 5-ounce boneless center-cut pork loin chops
- Vegetable oil spray

Directions:
1. Preheat the toaster oven to 350°F.
2. Set up and fill three shallow soup plates or small pie plates on your counter: one for the flour, one for the beaten egg(s), and one for the bread crumbs.
3. Dredge a pork chop in the flour, coating both sides as well as around the edge. Gently shake off any excess, then dip the chop in the egg(s), again coating both sides and the edge. Let any excess egg slip back into the rest, then set the chop in the bread crumbs, turning it and pressing gently to coat well on both sides and the edge. Coat the pork chop all over with vegetable oil spray and set aside so you can dredge, coat, and spray the additional chop(s).
4. Set the chops in the air fryer oven with as much air space between them as possible. Air-fry undisturbed for 12 minutes, or until brown and crunchy and an instant-read meat thermometer inserted into the center of a chop registers 145°F.
5. Use kitchen tongs to transfer the chops to a wire rack. Cool for 5 minutes before serving.

Kielbasa Chunks With Pineapple & Peppers

Servings: 2

Cooking Time: 10 Minutes

Ingredients:

- ¾ pound kielbasa sausage
- 1 cup bell pepper chunks (any color)
- 1 8-ounce can pineapple chunks in juice, drained
- 1 tablespoon barbeque seasoning
- 1 tablespoon soy sauce
- cooking spray

Directions:

1. Cut sausage into ½-inch slices.
2. In a medium bowl, toss all ingredients together.
3. Spray air fryer oven with nonstick cooking spray.
4. Pour sausage mixture into the air fryer oven.
5. Air-fry at 390°F for approximately 5 minutes. Cook an additional 5 minutes.

Indian Fry Bread Tacos

Servings: 4   Cooking Time: 20 Minutes

Ingredients:

- 1 cup all-purpose flour
- 1½ teaspoons salt, divided
- 1½ teaspoons baking powder
- ¼ cup milk
- ¼ cup warm water
- ½ pound lean ground beef
- One 14.5-ounce can pinto beans, drained and rinsed
- 1 tablespoon taco seasoning
- ½ cup shredded cheddar cheese
- 2 cups shredded lettuce
- ¼ cup black olives, chopped
- 1 Roma tomato, diced
- 1 avocado, diced
- 1 lime

Directions:

1. In a large bowl, whisk together the flour, 1 teaspoon of the salt, and baking powder. Make a well in the center and add in the milk and water. Form a ball and gently knead the dough four times. Cover the bowl with a damp towel, and set aside.
2. Preheat the toaster oven to 380°F.
3. In a medium bowl, mix together the ground beef, beans, and taco seasoning. Crumble the meat mixture into the air fryer oven and air-fry for 5 minutes; toss the meat and cook an additional 2 to 3 minutes, or until cooked fully. Place the cooked meat in a bowl for taco assembly; season with the remaining ½ teaspoon salt as desired.
4. On a floured surface, place the dough. Cut the dough into 4 equal parts. Using a rolling pin, roll out each piece of dough to 5 inches in diameter. Spray the dough with cooking spray and place in the air fryer oven, working in batches as needed. Air-fry for 3 minutes, flip over, spray with cooking spray, and air-fry for an additional 1 to 3 minutes, until golden and puffy.
5. To assemble, place the fry breads on a serving platter. Equally divide the meat and bean mixture on top of the fry bread. Divide the cheese, lettuce, olives, tomatoes, and avocado among the four tacos. Squeeze lime over the top prior to serving.

Kielbasa Sausage With Pierogies And Caramelized Onions

Servings: 3

Cooking Time: 30 Minutes

Ingredients:

- 1 Vidalia or sweet onion, sliced
- olive oil
- salt and freshly ground black pepper
- 2 tablespoons butter, cut into small cubes
- 1 teaspoon sugar
- 1 pound light Polish kielbasa sausage, cut into 2-inch chunks
- 1 (13-ounce) package frozen mini pierogies
- 2 teaspoons vegetable or olive oil
- chopped scallions

Directions:

1. Preheat the toaster oven to 400°F.
2. Toss the sliced onions with a little olive oil, salt and pepper and transfer them to the air fryer oven. Dot the onions with pieces of butter and air-fry at 400°F for 2 minutes. Then sprinkle the sugar over the onions and stir. Pour any melted butter from the bottom of the air fryer oven over the onions (do this over the sink – some of the butter will spill through the pan). Continue to air-fry for another 13 minutes, stirring the pan every few minutes to cook the onions evenly.
3. Add the kielbasa chunks to the onions and toss. Air-fry for another 5 minutes. Transfer the kielbasa and onions to a bowl and cover with aluminum foil to keep warm.
4. Toss the frozen pierogies with the vegetable or olive oil and transfer them to the air fryer oven. Air-fry at 400°F for 8 minutes.
5. When the pierogies have finished cooking, return the kielbasa and onions to the air fryer oven and gently toss with the pierogies. Air-fry for 2 more minutes and then transfer everything to a serving platter. Garnish with the chopped scallions and serve hot with the spicy sour cream sauce below.
6. Kielbasa Sausage with Pierogies and Caramelized Onions

Perfect Strip Steaks

Servings: 2

Cooking Time: 17 Minutes

Ingredients:
- 1½ tablespoons Olive oil
- 1½ tablespoons Minced garlic
- 2 teaspoons Ground black pepper
- 1 teaspoon Table salt
- 2 ¾-pound boneless beef strip steak(s)

Directions:
1. Preheat the toaster oven to 375°F (or 380°F or 390°F, if one of these is the closest setting).
2. Mix the oil, garlic, pepper, and salt in a small bowl, then smear this mixture over both sides of the steak(s).
3. When the machine is at temperature, put the steak(s) in the air fryer oven with as much air space as possible between them for the larger batch. They should not overlap or even touch. That said, even just a ¼-inch between them will work. Air-fry for 12 minutes, turning once, until an instant-read meat thermometer inserted into the thickest part of a steak registers 127°F for rare (not USDA-approved). Or air-fry for 15 minutes, turning once, until an instant-read meat thermometer registers 145°F for medium (USDA-approved). If the machine is at 390°F, the steaks may cook 2 minutes more quickly than the stated timing.
4. Use kitchen tongs to transfer the steak(s) to a wire rack. Cool for 5 minutes before serving.

Barbecue-style London Broil

Servings: 5

Cooking Time: 17 Minutes

Ingredients:
- ¾ teaspoon Mild smoked paprika
- ¾ teaspoon Dried oregano
- ¾ teaspoon Table salt
- ¾ teaspoon Ground black pepper
- ¼ teaspoon Garlic powder
- ¼ teaspoon Onion powder
- 1½ pounds Beef London broil (in one piece)
- Olive oil spray

Directions:
1. Preheat the toaster oven to 400°F.
2. Mix the smoked paprika, oregano, salt, pepper, garlic powder, and onion powder in a small bowl until uniform.
3. Pat and rub this mixture across all surfaces of the beef. Lightly coat the beef on all sides with olive oil spray.
4. When the machine is at temperature, lay the London broil flat in the air fryer oven and air-fry undisturbed for 8 minutes for the small batch, 10 minutes for the medium batch, or 12 minutes for the large batch for medium-rare, until an instant-read meat thermometer inserted into the center of the meat registers 130°F (not USDA-approved). Add 1, 2, or 3 minutes, respectively (based on the size of the cut) for medium, until an instant-read meat thermometer registers 135°F (not USDA-approved). Or add 3, 4, or 5 minutes respectively for medium, until an instant-read meat thermometer registers 145°F (USDA-approved).
5. Use kitchen tongs to transfer the London broil to a cutting board. Let the meat rest for 10 minutes. It needs a long time for the juices to be reincorporated into the meat's fibers. Carve it against the grain into very thin (less than ¼-inch-thick) slices to serve.

Printed in the USA
CPSIA information can be obtained
at www.ICGtesting.com
LVHW062039270823
756437LV00010B/1414